N.C. WYETH'S
MEN of CONCORD

April 15, 2016 – September 18, 2016

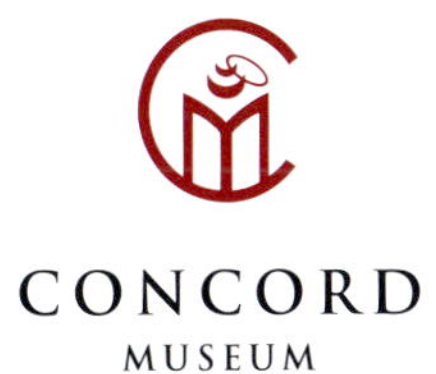

CONCORD
MUSEUM

ISBN: 978-0-9654145-3-1
Library of Congress Control Number: 2015920783

Published by Concord Museum
200 Lexington Road
Concord, Massachusetts 01742
www.concordmuseum.org

This publication has received major funding from:

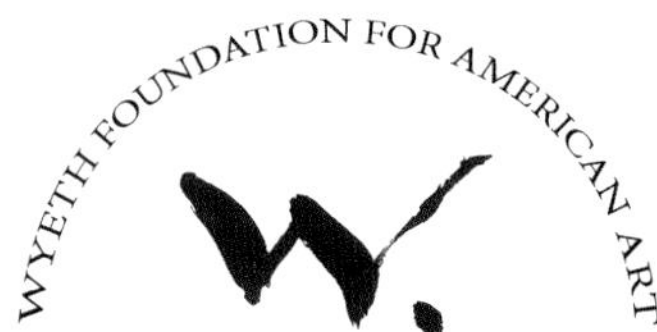

Front cover foldout: N. C. Wyeth, *Men of Concord,* endpaper illustration
Arkell Museum at Canajoharie, Gift of Bartlett Arkell, 1940

Back cover foldout: Interior of N. C. Wyeth's studio, Chadds Ford, Pennsylvania, photographer unknown, 1945, Wyeth Family Archives

Page 4: Henry D. Thoreau, by E. S. Dunshee, 1862, Concord Museum;
N. C. Wyeth painting in Chadds Ford, photographer unknown, about 1909, Wyeth Family Archives

Illustrations from *Men of Concord* by Henry David Thoreau

Catalogue designed by Jeffrey Williamson Design

CONTENTS

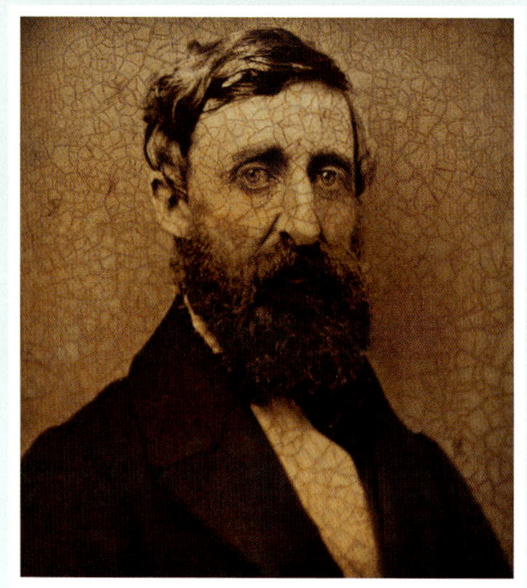

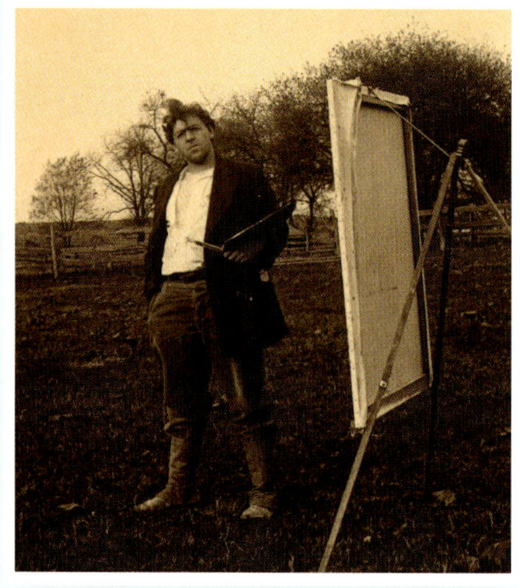

FOREWORD

The Concord Museum has long been renowned for its extraordinary Thoreau collection. As a fitting launch to the 2017 bicentennial of Henry Thoreau's birth, the Museum is pleased to present an exhibition that explores the meaningful and lifelong influence of the philosopher on the artist N. C. Wyeth.

The landmark exhibition *N. C. Wyeth's Men of Concord* has brought together for the first time in nearly eighty years the twelve original panels that Wyeth painted for the book *Men of Concord and Some Others, as Portrayed in the Journal of Henry David Thoreau.* We hope that the exhibition and this publication will shed new light on the artist's relationship to Concord and to Henry Thoreau and increase awareness of N. C. Wyeth's illustrious career.

The project represents a true collaboration between the Museum and the Concord Free Public Library, home to five of the twelve paintings. We are especially grateful to Sherry Litwack, President of the Concord Free Public Library Corporation, for her leadership and vision throughout project development. Concurrent with the Museum's exhibition, the Library's William Munroe Special Collections presents *From* Thoreau's Seasons *to* Men of Concord: *N. C. Wyeth Inspired.* This exhibition explores Wyeth's fascination with Thoreau by tracing the evolution of *Men of Concord* from Wyeth's initial inspiration to its triumphant 1936 publication.

The Concord Museum is indebted to the Wyeth Foundation for American Art for its generous support of this catalogue. We would also like to thank Lead Sponsor J. P. Morgan and the corporate and individual sponsors of the exhibition. We also extend our sincere gratitude to the many private lenders and public institutions that enabled us to unite once again the twelve paintings, together with related works. Finally, we thank the catalogue essayists: Christine B. Podmaniczky, Curator of N. C. Wyeth Collections and Historic Properties at the Brandywine River Museum of Art and Consulting Curator for *N. C. Wyeth's Men of Concord;* David F. Wood, Concord Museum Curator; and Leslie Perrin Wilson, Curator of the William Munroe Special Collections at the Concord Free Public Library. Through the work of these scholars, we have a deeper understanding of the profound influence that Henry Thoreau had on N. C. Wyeth.

MARGARET R. BURKE, Ph. D.
Executive Director, Concord Museum

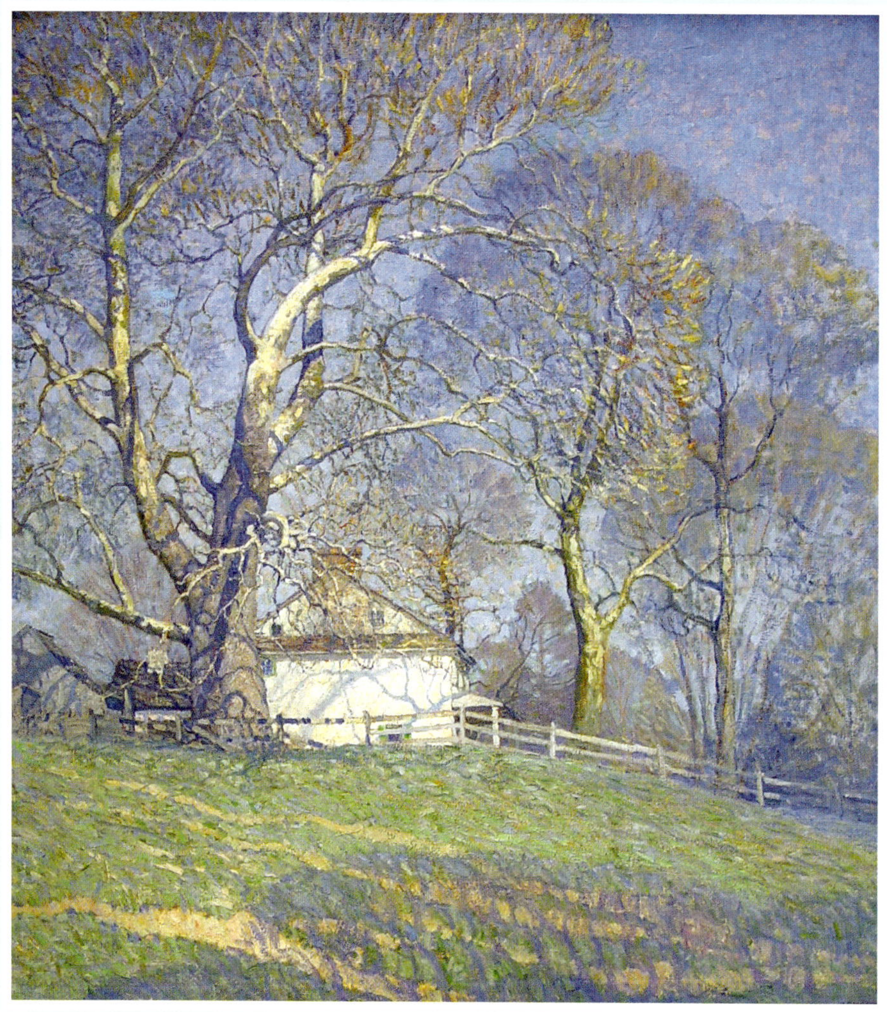

Buttonwood Farm

N. C. WYETH | 1920

Oil on canvas, 48½ x 42½ in. (123.2 x 107.9 cm)
Courtesy of Reading Public Museum, Reading, Pennsylvania
Gift of George D. Horst

N. C. WYETH, HENRY THOREAU, and the IMPORTANCE of PLACE

CHRISTINE B. PODMANICZKY

Curator, N. C. Wyeth Collections and Historic Properties, Brandywine River Museum of Art

"These are no mere perfunctory illustrations"—so the editor Francis H. Allen described the twelve pictures the renowned illustrator N. C. Wyeth created for *Men of Concord,* a volume of personal profiles drawn from the Journal of Henry David Thoreau. Allen, writing the book's preface in 1936, portrayed Wyeth as a "life-long admirer of Thoreau," an "intellectual disciple" whose character and work had been greatly influenced by the distinctly American philosopher and naturalist. Indeed, for almost three decades, Thoreau's writings informed, sustained, and inspired Wyeth, providing the artist with a remarkably sympathetic guide to his own quest for meaning in life and art. Wyeth was well known for the extensive research he undertook in preparation to illustrate the many books that bear his name. But the commission to illustrate *Men of Concord* was unique in his career. To no other project did he bring such a deeply rooted and personal connection with the subject, having read, studied, and lived with the writings of his "worshipped friend" for almost thirty years.[1]

Although Newell Convers Wyeth (1882–1945) grew up in Needham, Massachusetts, nearby Concord's literary history made no impression on him. In a late-in-life account of his boyhood and teen years, Wyeth specifically noted his early unfamiliarity with the writings of Henry David Thoreau. His introduction came in Wilmington, Delaware, where the twenty-year-old aspiring illustrator had gone to enroll in the Howard Pyle School of Art. In Wilmington he met Carolyn Bockius, whom he married in 1906, and it was the well-read Annie Brenneman Bockius who first introduced her son-in-law to Thoreau.[2] In Wyeth's extensive correspondence with his family, allusions to Thoreau's writings may be detected from late 1908 onward, when he began to fill his letters with visually rich descriptions of the landscape and natural phenomena; protests against the necessity of having a career; and musings on the difficult task of bringing himself into "perfect accord with the things around him in order to express powerful, harmonious, and perfect chords."[3]

Wyeth became a disciple of Thoreau in the spring of 1909. The first direct reference to Thoreau in his correspondence occurs in a letter written on

May 7, 1909: "I have just completed Thoreau's book." The unnamed book, probably *Walden,* cast a spell, and in mid-June that year Wyeth made the first of many pilgrimages to Walden Pond. Upon his return home, he wrote: "Somehow I feel that after reading Thoreau, becoming thoroughly imbued with his magnificent attitude toward nature, and then going to the very spot he loved and knew so intimately, I feel that it has intensified my attitude. . . . That trip to Concord was invaluable to me."[4]

Three books purchased in Concord document the trip and remain in Wyeth's studio library: *Thoreau: A Glimpse,* by Samuel Arthur Jones; *The Story of Concord Told by the Concord Writers,* by Josephine Latham Swayne; and a copy of *Walden,* each inscribed, "Concord, '09." Wyeth knew then that in Thoreau he would find honest, vital, and supportive text relevant to much of his own thinking. In September 1909 he read *Early Spring in Massachusetts,* a selection from the Journal that marked for him "the high water in the amount of comfort and inspiration." In March 1910 he was reading *Familiar Letters by Henry David Thoreau,* edited by F. B. Sanborn. By June 1912 he had acquired the twenty-volume set of *The Writings of Henry David Thoreau* "to be ever the source of deeper and deeper inspiration!"[5] In Thoreau, Wyeth had found himself.

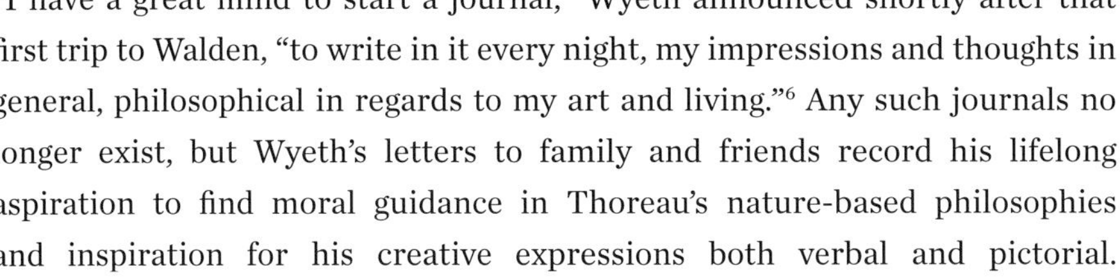

"I have a great mind to start a journal," Wyeth announced shortly after that first trip to Walden, "to write in it every night, my impressions and thoughts in general, philosophical in regards to my art and living."[6] Any such journals no longer exist, but Wyeth's letters to family and friends record his lifelong aspiration to find moral guidance in Thoreau's nature-based philosophies and inspiration for his creative expressions both verbal and pictorial. It was the wholeness of Thoreau's vision that appealed to Wyeth, who keenly felt, contemplated, and yearned to express the interconnection of life, art, and nature.

In Thoreau's writings Wyeth sought moral guidance "for almost every move [he could] make." On the endpapers of his copy of *Winter,* for example, he penciled notes and page numbers to readily refer to Thoreau's comments on issues with which he personally struggled. "The Devil and ourselves—351," he wrote, to index a passage on the presence of insidious temptations in daily life, while "virtue and publicity—362" marks Thoreau's assertion that "men should hear of your virtue only as they hear the creaking of the earth's axle and the music of the spheres." In his volumes Wyeth marked passages on a variety of subjects (such as wealth and poverty, social interaction, integrity), finding a code that appealed to him, a moral wisdom he recognized as "the foundation source of the arts in general, especially the art of life." Thoreau laid out "real tonics to brace a man when he is weary, to cleanse his vision until he sees the heights again"; Wyeth termed it pertinent, practical advice relevant to contemporary life.[7] Although at times throughout his life Wyeth would feel he had lost his way, he returned again and again to Thoreau's writings to regain balance.

In addition to moral guidance, in Thoreau's lyrical, romantic, almost painterly descriptions of his natural surroundings, Wyeth discovered a literary style that spoke to his own sensitivities and enriched his creativity. As he became familiar with Thoreau's writings, his letters to his family in Needham became, in part, his nature journals, closely chronicling his increasing awareness and appreciation of the natural world around him. His word pictures are as direct and visually luxuriant as Thoreau's, as in this excerpt, drawn from the description of a walk the artist took in search of motifs along a"musical stream, hidden, nearly always by the rank weed growths, young willow and high banks" adjacent to his property:

> *through clear, shallow, fast-running water, minnows darting either side of you at every step and frogs plunking in—sort of punctuating your steps—and then, as it happened with me to scare up a feeding blue heron and at intervals, disturbing the same pair of sand pipers that kept just so far ahead. . . . After I had left the brook's course, upon my return, (the sun indicating something after two), I gathered the first of the fall flowers including golden rod. There is a certain inexpressible pleasure in the very plucking of the brittle, pithy stems of fall flowers; they are so rank, so aromatic. My hands smelled of nuts and roots and all the things that flavor of the wholesome earth. And the blossoms themselves exude a sort of repressed fragrance, like herbs. I must have gathered some twenty varieties, including a great heavily laden spray of elderberry, fully ripe, the little sacks "plumpt with wine."*[8]

For decades Wyeth's letters would contain such vividly rich pictures of his natural surroundings, descriptions that proved that, like Thoreau, he savored the complete sensory assault of nature.

With Thoreau's example before him, Wyeth realized, however, that his finely tuned observations of the natural world were not an end in themselves but the impetus and framework for contemplation and self-examination: not just to learn about nature, but to learn from nature. Many of Wyeth's stunning descriptions of the landscape or weather conditions are followed by reflections on "the great intangible secrets of the universe." Wyeth believed these secrets were the basis for great art, and in his private painting he struggled throughout his career to capture on canvas a sense of ineffable truths.

It is no coincidence then that as he began to engage with Thoreau in the three or four years following 1909, the artist made several decisions that indelibly shaped his life, career, and the Wyeth legacy.

As a young illustrator, Wyeth had chosen Western and outdoor-themed action pictures as his specialty, traveling to Utah, Arizona, and New Mexico to seek authentic Western experiences as a foundation for his work. After a meteoric rise, by 1908 and 1909 he began to find the constraints and habits of illustration detrimental to his artistic development. He felt trapped, both by the artificiality of his Western work and by his choice of profession. His early readings in Thoreau validated the misgivings he was having regarding his career. "It is remarkable how easily and insensibly we fall into a particular route, and make a beaten track for ourselves," Thoreau wrote in *Walden*. Wyeth, for his part, felt he had "*bitched* [himself] with the accursed *success* in *skin*-deep pictures and illustrations," marking in his copy of Samuel Arthur Jones's *Thoreau: A Glimpse* Thoreau's claim that "the worst use you could put a man to was to set him to making money."[9] The artist would have preferred to give up illustration work altogether, but with a family to support he could only press art editors for more sympathetic commissions, particularly subjects that had local resonance, that he could paint honestly and conscientiously, directly from nature. While Wyeth continued to paint Western-themed pictures on occasion, he no longer styled himself a Western artist.

Between 1909 and 1912, as he deepened his acquaintance with Thoreau and the natural environment around him, Wyeth moved into landscape painting, searching to express in pigment observations and revelations he described in his letters. Convinced that true painting was the "result of a man's love, respect and knowledge of *nature,*" Wyeth set up his easel in nearby woods and fields to capture impressions that would further his grasp of both subject and craft.[10] Working on small canvases in a variety of impressionist styles, Wyeth sought to depict observed phenomena—particular light-and-shadow effects or atmospheric conditions—and he sampled a variety of techniques and styles in which to render his observations. *Chadds Ford Landscape—July 1909* (page 64) is one of the most successful of the group in the way the artist used subtle color and layered paint to achieve a sense of the heavy, humid air that softens the view to the horizon on a hot summer's day. Wyeth exhibited twenty-two of these paintings at the Philadelphia Sketch Club in 1912 (with titles such as *Sultry Day, Gray Day, February,* and *Rain*), but the generally loose, almost unfinished appearance of many ensured that the group was not critically well received. Wyeth knew he had set himself a daunting task: "Such effects as I have seen the past three days—any one of them painted as I saw and felt them," he wrote after particularly unsettled weather in late January 1909, "would make a reputation for a man;—but then, one has to know how to do it!"[11]

Despite the frustrations he encountered, he counseled his fellow artists to study nature rather than the work of other artists. "For truth in painting," he told his fellow Pyle graduate Allen Tupper True, "go to nature. . . . Get close to nature first; that comes only by studying her secrets." Painters came to Chadds Ford, Wyeth wrote, "like hunters with guns over their shoulders," to "shoot landscapes" and nothing more. They talked of "beautiful brooks," "lovely trees," "wonderful skies," "bully atmosphere," but he felt they had no "appreciation of the deeper significance of growing things, of the mystery of nature, of its *deeper* meaning."[12] Thoreau's writings validated and strengthened the faith Wyeth placed in the power of the natural world; his real painting, he felt, was evidenced in those canvases in which he explored man's place within that world. Though his impressionist efforts were largely unsatisfactory, he continued throughout his career to search for the most effective expression of his love, respect, and knowledge of nature.

The importance Thoreau assigned to one's specific locality appealed strongly to Wyeth and no doubt reinforced the artist's decision to settle in the small town of Chadds Ford, in southeastern Pennsylvania. "To be deep-rooted in a country is all-essential," the artist wrote of the beautiful countryside he had come to know as a student in Howard Pyle's summer classes. In 1911 the artist purchased eighteen acres on the south face of Rocky Hill, a site less than a mile from the village, calling it "the little corner of the world wherein [he] would work out [his] destiny." From his home he could see the Brandywine River and the distant hills beyond, the village and the surrounding farmlands, the railroad line, and a Revolutionary War battleground. Chadds Ford would become his Walden. "Here," he wrote, "my soul comes nearer to the surface than [in] any place I know." No disciple of Thoreau would better succeed in planting roots that nourished two subsequent generations of artists equally intimate with the force of locality.[13]

"If these fields and streams and woods, the phenomena of nature here . . . should cease to interest and inspire me, no culture or wealth would atone for the loss," Thoreau wrote in his Journal. The passage resonated with the artist, and he often quoted or paraphrased it. "I find," the artist confessed, "that I know so little of my own back-yard" that he had little reason to "travel afar" for motifs. In *Walden* Wyeth would have read Thoreau's assertion that "though the view from my door was still more contracted, I did not feel crowded or confined in the least." In a similar mind, Wyeth allowed, "I am just beginning to see *big* things out of my studio door. . . . It used to be I thought the outlook . . . *common-place* from an artistic standpoint—*Now* I see endless opportunities."[14] For the artist, this focus on the microcosm of one's immediate environment (a mindset he also took to his summer property in Maine) remained a lifelong tenet.

Wyeth never traveled abroad—both he and Thoreau feared "the dissipation that traveling [implied]." He cultivated a prodigious imagination, however, and, like Thoreau, though he limited himself geographically, his imaginative powers richly nourished his art. He too found "pasture enough" for his imagination in his immediate surroundings. From Concord, Thoreau imagined "the prairies of the West and the steppes of Tartary," whereas Wyeth found the sycamore trees and the rolling hills of the Brandywine country stood well for Sherwood Forest or Arthurian England.[15]

The strength of these ties was tested in 1921, when Wyeth moved his family to Needham, lured in part by a promise from Houghton Mifflin to illustrate a selection from Thoreau's Journal. The whole family recognized its deep commitment to Chadds Ford, and by 1923 the Wyeths had returned to Pennsylvania, the Thoreau project postponed. "A man dwells in his native valley like a corolla in its calyx, like an acorn in its cup. *Here*, of course, is all that you love, all that you expect, all that you are," wrote Thoreau in a Journal passage that reflects Wyeth's commitment to his natural and social community.[16]

Wyeth's personality was such that he could not but proselytize for Thoreau, at a time when the sage of Walden was considered "a crusty old hack" who produced "dry, dusty . . . categorical notes . . . of birds, flowers and trees."[17] He urged his family and friends to meet Thoreau as he had, and he gave copies of his favorite books to anyone he felt would benefit. For Christmas 1909, to his brother Edwin, a Harvard student, he gave a "pocket leather bound edition" of *Early Spring in Massachusetts,* with the inscription, "I'll warrant that this book . . . will supply a form of vital education not to be found in the world's best universities." To his brother Stimson, serving with the army in France during Christmas 1917, he sent another copy of *Early Spring in Massachusetts.* And in 1916 and 1917, when Wyeth taught painting to four students in Chadds Ford, the regular Sunday-night sessions were given over to readings from Thoreau.

Even though the Concord writer was undervalued or largely ignored in both philosophical and literary assessments, Wyeth welcomed every opportunity to introduce Thoreau to colleagues or to discuss Thoreau with those few fellow admirers he happened upon. In 1912, shortly after meeting the art critic Christian Brinton (1870–1942), Wyeth sent Brinton a volume of Thoreau's writings, with an apology for the distraction of his page markings. He hoped Brinton would recognize Thoreau's "practical value to the world, . . . in this age of headless living and mad dashes from one ephemeral sensation to another."[18] In February 1918 a chance meeting on a train with the poet Edwin Markham (1852–1940), whom Wyeth described as "an ardent and enthusiastic student of Thoreau," left him feeling "much more convinced of Thoreau's vitality and greatness." From Markham, Wyeth learned about Lafcadio Hearn (Koizumi Yakumo, 1850–1904), an author who had succeeded in making the Japanese "more vitally concerned with the doctrines of Walden's sage than we are," thus accounting for an influx of Japanese tourists Wyeth had noticed at Walden the year before.[19] And at nearby West Chester State Normal School, he discussed Thoreau with the scholar Francis H. Green (1861–1951), who impressed him with a collection of original Thoreau material.[20]

Throughout his life, Wyeth took every opportunity to counter the prevalent image of Thoreau as an amateur naturalist and to emphasize "the strong human appeal of the poet, the dramatist, the stoic, the mystic—the magnificent romance of the man." On January 18, 1920, Wyeth gave a talk titled "Thoreau, His Critics and the Public" at a meeting of the Lantern Club in Wilmington, a group of fellow artists, civic leaders, and businessmen. Wyeth hoped to place "a shot here and there" among the "rich dilettantes," his aim, as always, to underscore his belief that Thoreau offered real and sorely needed insight "in this leveling and tragical age."

As he worked on his lecture, the artist was moved in that same week to finish a canvas he had started the preceding spring, a view of a Revolutionary War–era house surrounded by huge sycamore trees sited on the nearby Brandywine battlefield. Wyeth's painting of "the towering sycamore brilliant with light and trembling in the breeze always" is the result of close observation, a Thoreauvian-style discipline that generated the insight and intimacy that allowed him to present the tree's beauty and impressiveness.[21] The painting (page 6) is one of Wyeth's finest Brandywine landscapes.

After decades of advocating in correspondence and conversation for the relevancy of Thoreau's philosophies and the inspirational value of his nature writings, in 1932 Wyeth finally created a painting depicting Thoreau at Walden Pond. *Walden Pond Revisited* (page 66) is a large canvas inspired by the artist's repeated outings to the sacred site. In these emotionally charged visits, Wyeth intensely sensed the spirit of Thoreau; in his painting he created a spectral-like figure looming over the Walden landscape, an attempt to visually communicate the mysticism and romance he personally associated with Thoreau. The painting is a complete catalogue of Thoreauvian symbols and now seems heavy-handed, even campy; in the mid-1930s, however, it presented a basic invitation to a largely unaware public.

Just a few years later, as Wyeth planned the illustrative program for *Men of Concord,* he took a different approach, recalling perhaps an article he had written for the *New York Times* in October 1912. As an example of the perfect harmony between text and image, he had cited his recently acquired edition of *The Writings,* illustrated with photogravures "of Thoreau's country" by Herbert W. Gleason. "There was," he noted, "no attempt to match [Thoreau's] descriptions or thoughts, and yet [the photogravures] added a note both charming and vital to his diary; passive symbols of the woods, fields, and streams so profoundly loved and understood by the great philosopher." Gleason's images represented to him the "the purest kind of illustration."[22] Wyeth brought to the *Men of Concord* project almost thirty years of close study, yet he chose simple subjects, honestly painted in a forthright style. The illustrations touch lightly on Thoreau's text —figures such as Barefooted Brooks Clark, the pickerel fishermen, and Cyrus Hubbard with his ox team have no starring roles in Thoreau's account; neither is the action heroic by dramatic standards, being confined to conversation, contemplation, and craft. Inspired by his abiding respect and affection for Thoreau, Wyeth's men of Concord appear accessible, authentic, and engaging, visually drawing the reader into the Thoreauvian world valued for so long by the artist.

NOTES

1. N. C. Wyeth (NCW) to Henriette Zirngiebel Wyeth (HZW), March 13, 1912. Unless otherwise noted, this and all subsequent quotations from letters are from the Wyeth Family Archives, private collection, Chadds Ford, Pa.

2. David Michaelis, *N. C. Wyeth: A Biography* (New York: Knopf, 1998), p. 95. Wyeth occasionally asserted that his maternal grandfather, the botanist John Denys Zirngiebel, knew Thoreau, but Michaelis found no substantiation for the claim.

3. NCW to Andrew Newell Wyeth Jr., February 20, 1909.

4. NCW to HZW, July 6, 1909.

5. "Spring," NCW to Stimson Wyeth, September 1, 1909; *"Familiar,"* NCW to "Dear Folks," March 25, 1910; *"Writings,"* NCW to Stimson Wyeth, June 30, 1912. The whereabouts of Wyeth's first set of *The Writings* is unknown; it was replaced in 1935 by a set of the Manuscript Edition, no. 281 (Boston: Houghton Mifflin, 1906), which remains in Wyeth's library (Brandywine River Museum of Art, N. C. Wyeth House and Studio Collection).

6. NCW to HZW, July 16, 1909.

7. "For almost every," NCW to HZW, December 10, 1914; "foundation" and "real tonics," N. C. Wyeth, "Thoreau, His Critics and the Public," *Thoreau Society Bulletin 37* (October 1951): unpaginated.

8. NCW to HZW, August 15, 1909.

9. Thoreau, *The Writings,* 2:355; NCW to Sidney M. Chase, April 15, 1914; Samuel Arthur Jones, *Thoreau: A Glimpse* (Concord: Albert Lane, The Erudite Press, 1903); NCW's copy (Brandywine River Museum of Art, N. C. Wyeth House and Studio Collection) is marked on p. 16 regarding the necessity to earn money.

10. NCW to HZW, October 15, 1909.

11. *Exhibition of Landscapes and Original Illustrations by N. C. Wyeth,* Philadelphia Sketch Club, November 4–23, 1912, brochure collection of Christian C. Sanderson Museum, Chadds Ford, Pa.; "such effects," NCW to HZW, January 22, 1909.

12. NCW to Allen True, January 6, 1909, Allen Tupper True Papers, Archives of American Art, roll no. 4894, frame 1118–1124; "like hunters" and following, NCW to HZW, April 10, 1908.

13. "To be," NCW to HZW, December 5, 1908; "little corner" and "my soul," NCW to "Dear Folks," March 7, 1911. Coincidentally, Wyeth's son Andrew, another artist whose work was profoundly rooted in locality, was born exactly one hundred years to the day after Thoreau.

14. "If these fields," Thoreau, *The Writings*, 14:204; "though the view," Thoreau, *The Writings,* 2:97; "I find" and "I am just," NCW to HZW, August 15, 1909.

15. "Dissipation," Thoreau, *The Writings,* 14:204; "pasture" and "prairies," ibid., 2:97.

16. Thoreau, *The Writings,* 17:275.

17. NCW, "Thoreau, His Critics and the Public," n.p.

18. NCW to Christian Brinton, draft letter dated "Studio, Saturday morning" and found inserted in NCW's copy of Jones, *Thoreau: A Glimpse,* Brandywine River Museum of Art, N. C. Wyeth House and Studio Collection.

19. NCW to HZW, February 14, 1918.

20. NCW to HZW, dated "Studio/Friday" and filed after August 29, 1918.

21. NCW to HZW, August 15, 1909.

22. NCW, "On Illustrations: A Suggestion and a Comment on Illustrating Fiction," *New York Times*, October 13, 1912, p. 574.

June 30, 1912

my mind, ever surging and crowding as inspiration followed inspiration in quick succession, ~~urged~~ stirred to even faster conception by the sounds of birds, the flying clouds, the summer smells of ripened grass, tansy and wild carrot and over all, the throbbing bees, and flicker there of sparkling summer colors! But that dear old Master of divine philosophy presented me with answers manifold! And Babe! to think ~~that~~ I have them <u>all</u> at my service — <u>twenty</u> <u>volumes</u>! to be read my life long — to be ever the source of deeper and deeper inspiration!

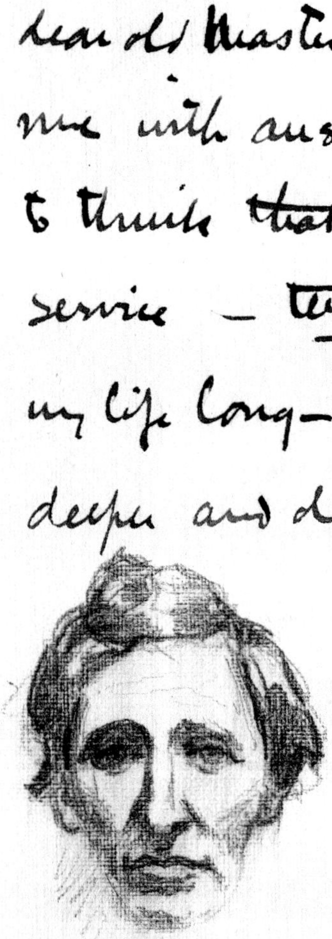

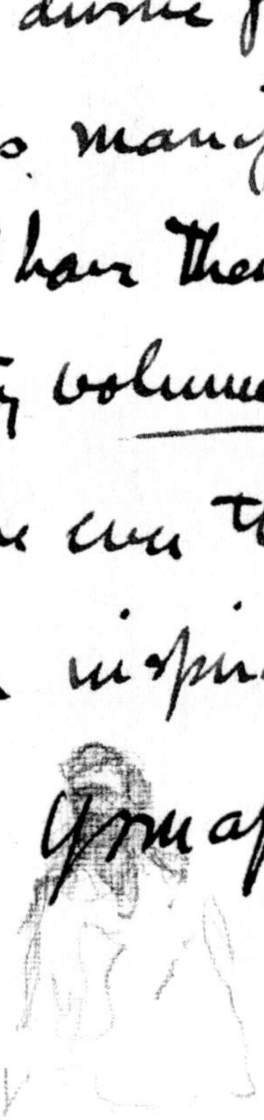

Your affectionate brother
Cowan.

GETTING a LIVING

DAVID F. WOOD
Curator, Concord Museum

The best of Thoreau is in his "Journals." — Odell Shepard, 1927

Henry Thoreau is best known as the author of *Walden*, and it may well be by way of *Walden* that most readers today encounter him. Nevertheless, many serious Thoreau scholars will enthusiastically echo Odell Shepard; if you want to discover one of the greatest American minds of the nineteenth century, the brilliant and wide-ranging intellect that was Henry Thoreau, look for him in his Journal.

Thoreau commented frequently about his Journal in the Journal itself, which he began in 1837. In 1840 he inscribed what reads like a bedtime prayer for his Journal: "Let the daily tide leave some deposit on these pages" (July 4, 1840).[1] It is as if Thoreau saw the keeping of a journal as somehow mysterious and to a degree involuntary. Six months later, it was still mysterious: "Of all the strange and unaccountable things this journalizing is the strangest" (January 29, 1841). Not long after, Thoreau recorded a partial conclusion about what his Journal was, or perhaps what it was not: "My Journal is that of me which would else spill over and run to waste" (February 8, 1841). Ten years later came another sort of conclusion, stating not what the Journal was but what it should be: "My Journal should be the record of my love" (November 16, 1851).

Thoreau consistently avoided putting boundaries around his Journal, but over time the uses he made of it changed. For more than a decade after he began it, Thoreau treated his Journal in part as a resource to be cut up and reassembled into other projects, such as lyceum lectures and essays for publication. Over time he abandoned this practice. Early in 1852 he wrote what amounts (almost) to an emancipation proclamation for the Journal: "I do not know but thoughts written down thus in a journal might be printed in the same form with greater advantage than if the related ones were brought together into separate essays" (January 27, 1852).

Thoreau's thoughts do show to great advantage in his Journal; as Odell Shepard put it, it is the best of Thoreau. Shepard's quote is from his introduction to a compilation of extracts from what finally amounted to the two million words of Thoreau's Journal. *The Heart of Thoreau's Journals* was published nine years before *Men of Concord*, but nine years before that, in 1918, N. C. Wyeth had already expressed his own appreciation of the value of coming to know Thoreau by way of his Journal when he proposed to the publisher Houghton Mifflin that it issue an illustrated volume of Journal extracts. That proposal was finally realized, in 1936, as *Men of Concord*.[2] The specific passages Wyeth chose for illustration in *Men of Concord* suggest that among the subjects he focused on in his reading of the Journal was one particularly important to painter and writer alike: vocation, or as Thoreau often termed it, getting a living. Several of N. C. Wyeth's illustrations for *Men of Concord* represent passages that deal, directly or indirectly, with the matter of vocation.

The problem of getting a living concerned Thoreau for most of his life. One of his proposed solutions was to reduce demand; rather than dig ditches to get money for tea, he advised in *Walden*, don't drink tea. But the problem goes well beyond subsistence; Thoreau wanted to know the best use he could make of his life, and he encouraged others to earnestly seek for the best use to make of their own lives. Often enough, the term Thoreau used as expressive of the highest purpose in his life was *poet*. For N. C. Wyeth, it was *artist*.[3]

The subject of *The Carpenters Repairing Hubbard's Bridge* (page 39) is the Journal passage for August 17, 1851. Here Thoreau performs a few variations on the theme "All men's employments, all trades and professions, in some of their aspects are attractive." He cites a boy he knew who, "having sucked cider at a minister's cider-mill, resolved to be a minister"; the boy was "willing to purchase that pleasure at any price." The work on Hubbard's Bridge, which goes over the Sudbury River on the way to Nine Acre Corner, similarly inspired Thoreau: "When I saw the carpenters the other day repairing Hubbard's Bridge, their bench on the new planking they had laid over the water in the sun and air, with no railing yet to obstruct the view, I was almost ready to resolve that I would be a carpenter and work on bridges, to secure a pleasant place to work." An added attraction was the fish line one of the men looked at from time to time. In a related passage a week later (August 23, 1851) Thoreau inverts the thought and reproaches himself for not paying *enough* attention to the employments of men, for not seeing more poetry in them, which was of course his real employment.

The Journal entry for May 6, 1854, is the subject of *The Muskrat-Hunters, Goodwin and Haynes* (page 47). In his image Wyeth followed almost verbatim the small, tense drama Thoreau's passage narrated: "One in [the] stern paddling slowly along, while the other sat with his gun ready cocked and the dog erect in the prow, all eyes constantly scanning the surface." The standing figure is John Goodwin, "the one-eyed Ajax," as Thoreau once called him in recognition of his physical strength; the seated figure is Sudbury Haynes. Thoreau was generally pleased to encounter Goodwin in the Concord landscape, "though he is regarded by most as a vicious character" (October 22, 1853); he concluded that "Goodwin cannot be a very bad man, he is so cheery" (November 27, 1858). Thoreau happily shared the Concord woods with hunters, fishermen, and woodcutters, enjoyed speaking with them, and wrote of their mode of living sympathetically. Of another of these sportsmen, George Melvin, like Goodwin a muskrat hunter and fisherman, Thoreau wrote, "He follows hunting, praise be to him, as regularly in our tame fields as the farmers follow farming" (December 2, 1856).

In the late fall of 1853 Thoreau came upon "one-eyed John Goodwin the fisherman" gathering firewood from the river. "It was a beautiful evening—& a clear amber sunset lit up all the eastern shores," he wrote in his Journal, and he went on to compare "that man's employment so simple & direct" to the "pursuits of most men—so artificial and complicated" (October 22, 1853). Five years later Thoreau came upon Goodwin again gathering firewood, this time by grubbing up stumps, and "helped him tip over a stump or two." Thoreau returned to his theme, which is at heart a critique of Adam Smith, asking again whether it is better to work in the city at a job you don't especially like in order to afford your firewood, or to spend your time gathering it yourself from cut-over woodlots or the river. Thoreau preferred to observe the latter, certainly, and even practiced it himself, "But, strange to say, the town does not like to have him [Goodwin] get his fuel in this way. . . . They have almost without dissent agreed on a different mode of living, with their division of labor" (November 4, 1858).

In the Journal passage that *Mr. Alcott in the Granary Burying Ground in Boston* (page 43) illustrates, Thoreau takes his friend Bronson Alcott—"The sanest man I ever knew" (May 9, 1853)—to task for, essentially, choosing avocation over vocation. Thoreau liberally sprinkles this Journal entry with exclamation points to signal his astonishment that Alcott, "He, the spiritual philosopher . . . He who wrote of Human Culture, he who conducted the Conversations on the Gospels, he who discoursed of Sleep, Health, Worship, Friendship" should devote himself to wills and epitaphs "with the zeal of a professed antiquarian and genealogist!" (August 11, 1852).

The matter of getting a living was unquestionably a concern for Bronson Alcott. Thoreau wrote of Alcott in a Journal entry almost exactly one year later: "The question of a livelihood was troubling him. He knew of nothing which he could do for which men would pay him" (August 10, 1853). Manual labor was not a viable option: "He could not compete with the Irish in cradling grain"; nor was office work: "His early education had not fitted him for a clerkship." Thoreau noted disgustedly that Alcott was denied a post that was particularly well suited to him—spokesman for the American Abolition Society—because he was overqualified: "They [William Lloyd Garrison and Wendell Phillips] cannot tolerate a man who stands by a head above them."

Two of the plates, *Thoreau Fishing* (page 37) and *Fishing Through the Ice* (page 49), are directly about fishing. Thoreau gave no small amount of thought to fishing; he had "skill at it, and a certain instinct for it";[4] and he allowed that fishing had given him "such simple joy . . . as might inspire the muse of Homer or Shakspeare" (July 7, 1840). But he also admitted, "I find I cannot fish without falling a little in my own respect."[5] Still, he had an unquestionable sympathy for those who pursued the fish in Concord's streams and ponds, and he also had something to say about the role fishing might play not just in getting a living, but in advancing the greater goal of living ethically.

A Journal passage from early June 1850 demonstrates Thoreau's ambivalence toward fishing and is the subject of *Thoreau Fishing.* In this image Wyeth depicts Thoreau in the quiet absorption typical of fishing, but in fact the Journal entry is about the notorious occasion on which he set the Concord woods on fire. Although Thoreau was able to rationalize his role in the affair, somewhat dubiously, as being equivalent to the role lightning plays in forest fires, he also admitted that "the trivial fishing was all that disturbed me and disturbs me still."[6]

Fishing Through the Ice falls between pages 131 and 132 of the 1936 edition of *Men of Concord,* as if it were meant to illustrate the Journal passage dated February 8, 1856. While that passage does refer to ice fishing—"Some think it best to cut the holes the day before"—Wyeth's illustration seems instead to be drawn at least partially from a Journal passage that isn't among those included in *Men of Concord:* "As I enter on Fair Haven Pond, I see already three pickerel-fishers retreating from it, drawing a sled through the Baker Farm, and see where they have been fishing, by the shining chips of ice about the holes" (December 7, 1856).

This passage and several other, similar Journal passages are about the men of Concord, John Goodwin prominent among them, for whom fishing is not just a sport but part of their livelihood. "I hear Goodwin had some fish to dispose of," Thoreau wrote on Christmas Day, 1859; "probably not more than a dollar's worth, however." Like the gathering of free-range firewood, the gathering of wild fish was criticized, even if sometimes hypocritically: "Some fisherman or other is ready with his reels and bait as soon as the ice will bear, whether it be Saturday or Sunday. Theirs, too, is a sort of devotion, though it be called hard names by the preacher. . . . Perhaps he dines off their pickerel on Monday at the hotel" (December 7, 1856).

But Thoreau also acknowledged a virtue to fishing that might overcome its drawbacks and even recommend it as a proper way of getting a living: "It tempts me as one means of becoming acquainted with nature; not only with fishes but with night & water and the scenery."[7] Thoreau was willing to imagine that this virtue belonged to fishing itself, no matter who did the angling. On the Sunday after Christmas in 1856, he noted: "Goodwin & Co. are fishing there [Walden Pond] today. . . . The fishermen sit by their damp fire of rotten pine wood . . . and, if not catching many fish, still getting what they went for, though they may not be aware of it, i.e. a wilder experience than the town affords" (December 28, 1856).

Thoreau addressed the matter of vocation many times in his Journal—for instance, in an entry dated June 15, 1852: "The motive of the laborer should be not to get a living, to get a good job, but to perform well a certain work." The subject may be fairly said to pervade the Journal, to such a degree that it really can't be missed by an attentive reader. N. C. Wyeth gave Henry Thoreau a great deal of his attention, and the specific choices he made in selecting passages to illustrate in *Men of Concord* may indicate that the lesson was not lost on him.

NOTES

Page 16: Letter with pencil drawing, N. C. Wyeth to Stimson Wyeth, June 30, 1912, courtesy Wyeth Family Archives.

1. The dates in parentheses are those of the Journal passage cited. In many cases these entries can be found in *Men of Concord* or in *The Heart of Thoreau's Journals*. All can be found in the Dover edition of the 1906 *Walden Edition of the Works of Henry Thoreau*. The Thoreau Institute has an online version of the 1906 edition that is searchable by date: www.walden.org/Library/The_Writings_of_Henry_David_Thoreau:_The_Digital_Collection/Journal.

2. See pp. 23–27 in this catalogue.

3. See pp. 7–15 in this catalogue.

4. *The Writings of Henry D. Thoreau: Journal*, vol. 2, *1842–1848* (Princeton: Princeton University Press, 1984), 241 (after April 18, 1846).

5. Ibid.

6. *The Writings of Henry D. Thoreau; Journal*, vol. 3, *1848–1851* (Princeton: Princeton University Press, 1990), 78 (after May 31, 1850).

7. Thoreau, *The Writings*, 2:241 (after April 18, 1846).

134-6

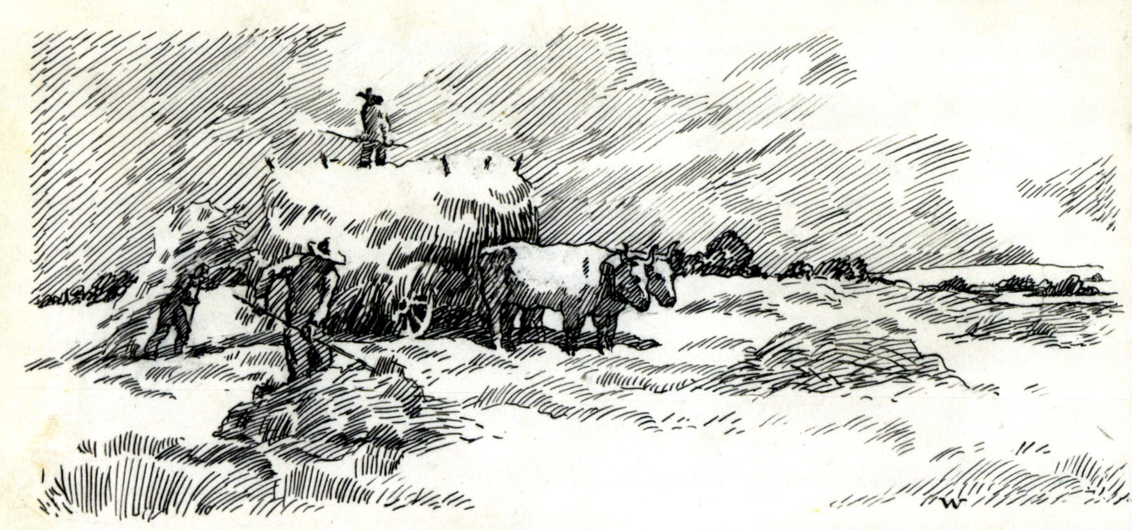

4' 1/4" base

#1148

~~#874 Wed noon~~

Blue Print

MEN OF CONCORD
HAYING
AUG 17th — Galley 17

EVOLUTION of MEN of CONCORD

LESLIE PERRIN WILSON

Curator, William Munroe Special Collections
Concord Free Public Library

For forty years, N. C. Wyeth was inspired by Henry David Thoreau. His fascination with the author crested with the 1936 book *Men of Concord,* a selection of entries from Thoreau's Journal with color illustrations by Wyeth and pen-and-ink sketches by his son Andrew. The book was Wyeth's brainchild, to which the Boston publishing firm Houghton Mifflin committed only reluctantly. Once conceived, it was slow to materialize, caught between Wyeth's "irresistible desire" to start it and his grueling workload as one of America's most successful illustrators.[1]

Late in 1918 Houghton Mifflin asked Wyeth to illustrate an edition of Hawthorne's *Grandfather's Chair.* The artist had earlier provided the company with illustrations for Mary Johnston's *The Long Roll* and *Cease Firing* (published in 1911 and 1912). When offered the Hawthorne project, he expressed polite pleasure at the idea of working with Houghton Mifflin again. But he declined the Hawthorne book, which he found "perfunctory and spiritless."[2]

In a December 14, 1918, letter to Julia Starkey at Houghton Mifflin, he seized the opportunity to pitch another project much closer to his heart. As a devotee of Thoreau, he knew that Houghton Mifflin—a descendant of Ticknor and Fields, which issued the first edition of *Walden* in 1854—was the traditional publisher of the author's writings. It was a great ambition of his, he wrote, "to paint in mural form, either in a book or upon the walls of some building a series of interpretations of this author[']s message as expressed in his works and in his life."[3] He suggested a book of illustrated entries from Thoreau's Journal, the text to be drawn from Harrison Gray Otis Blake's four volumes of journal selections, organized by season and published by Houghton Mifflin late in the nineteenth century.

Wyeth had been born and raised in Needham, Massachusetts, near Thoreau's beloved Concord, but he discovered Thoreau only after he became a student of the illustrator Howard Pyle in Wilmington, Delaware. The author's life and writings resonated with Wyeth, who declared in 1911, "The subtle and glorious glimpse into the life and soul of Thoreau is marvelous and means exceedingly more to me than the Bible and the works of all other men, dead and alive, put together!"[4]

He elevated Thoreau as an ethical and spiritual guide and a creative influence. Conflicted by the materialism and commercialism that drove his career as an illustrator, he clung to Thoreau's embrace of simplicity and the integrity of his life and writings. Dismayed by the common apprehension of his idol as little more than an amateur naturalist, Wyeth was eager to convince others of the coherence of the various aspects of Thoreau's work—observations of nature and philosophical and spiritual explorations—as well as of his essential humanity.

Julia Starkey saw the potential for a "chef d'oeuvre" in Wyeth's suggestion, but Roger Livingston Scaife (a director at Houghton Mifflin) showed less enthusiasm.[5] On December 22, 1918, Wyeth took Scaife to task for the "dampening effect" of the company's attitude on potential readers.[6] He criticized the tendency to pigeonhole Thoreau as a writer for nature lovers only. Pulling out all the stops in an effort to bring Scaife to a proper appreciation of Thoreau, he described the author's specific observations of nature as the "opalescent tapestry against which the jewels from his profound brain sparkle and glisten."[7]

Chastened, Scaife responded: "You are right. If you are so thoroughly imbued with the spirit of Thoreau you ought by all means to have the opportunity of paying your tribute to him by illustrating his work, and we will revise our opinion and gladly meet yours."[8] He urged Wyeth to make selections from Thoreau's Journal and to plan the physical aspects of the book, which would be published on the half-profit plan (meaning that after expenses were met, Wyeth and Houghton Mifflin would each get half the profits). Scaife thus gave Wyeth both great freedom and, at the same time, an accompanying level of responsibility that the illustrator would be unable to meet while simultaneously accepting and carrying out other professional obligations.

The Thoreauvian Francis Henry Allen, a longtime member of the Houghton Mifflin editorial staff, was soon apprised of Wyeth's proposed book. Allen had coedited with Bradford Torrey the fourteen volumes of Thoreau's Journal published by Houghton Mifflin in 1906 as volumes 7–20 of the Manuscript and Walden Editions of *The Writings of Henry David Thoreau.* Houghton Mifflin had also published his *Bibliography of Henry David Thoreau* and *Notes on New England Birds.*

On January 25, 1919, Wyeth wrote to Allen that the book would constitute "a sort of Thoreau propaganda."[9] Allen had proposed that Wyeth pick journal entries from the 1906 text rather than Blake's selections, and Wyeth reported that he had already begun to do so, for the reason that the 1906 edition included most of the Journal, unlike Blake's earlier volumes. The book would be titled *Thoreau's Seasons* and would be arranged by the seasons of the year.

Although neither Wyeth nor Allen could have known it in 1919, Allen would ultimately play a major role in realizing the book according to a quite different plan.

Impatient though Wyeth was to work on the Thoreau book, he had ongoing projects with Scribner's and Cosmopolitan Book. Moreover, Houghton Mifflin had barely agreed to publish *Thoreau's Seasons* when, in March 1919, it asked him to tackle an edition of Longfellow's *Courtship of Miles Standish.* On July 12, 1920, Wyeth begged Scaife not to distract him with additional illustrative work until the Thoreau volume was published. Regardless, the company offered him George Herbert Palmer's translation of the *Odyssey.* With a national reputation and a popular following, he had his pick of more illustrative and other commissioned work than he could possibly take on. He never lost interest in *Thoreau's Seasons,* but the possibility of bringing it into existence seemed always just out of reach. The wake-up call came in 1927.

During the 1920s Houghton Mifflin had begun to recognize a rising market for a Thoreau selection for a general audience. Having little to show for years of thinking about his cherished project, wWyeth was dismayed to learn of the company's publication in 1927 of *The Heart of Thoreau's Journals,* edited by the the academic, author, and poet Odell Shepard. Wyeth wrote to Roger Scaife, "Like many of the things close to my heart, this glorious opportunity was necessarily and constantly postponed—and now it is done."[10]

Scaife hastened to boost Wyeth's spirits: "The fact that we have brought together Thoreau's philosophy of life in one volume ought to be but a beginning."[11] Scaife was prescient in framing Shepard's book as a harbinger of rising twentieth-century interest in Thoreau. His optimism cheered Wyeth.

Wyeth's illustrated Thoreau book finally began to take form in 1930, when Francis Allen plucked editorial responsibility from the artist's hands. On December 3 Allen sent a memorandum to Ferris Greenslet—a Houghton Mifflin director and later general manager of the company's trade division—to tell him of his own interest in making a selection from Thoreau, "to consist entirely of character sketches and bits of narrative to bring out his knowledge of human nature."[12] Allen listed some of the Concord personalities who might be included and matched them with citations to specific journal passages. He mentioned Wyeth's stalled Thoreau project and observed that the book he had in mind "would lend itself to illustration by such an artist as Wyeth."[13]

Houghton Mifflin embraced Allen's idea, and *Thoreau's Seasons* was transformed into *Men of Concord,* despite Wyeth's objections to the new title. Allen's involvement reduced Wyeth's role in the book, introduced another approach to Thoreau, and required abandoning the seasonal organization scheme. If Wyeth felt a sense of loss, the result was still a published Thoreau volume illustrated by him—an outcome that might never have been achieved had Allen not interjected himself into the process.

Wyeth did not begin the panels for *Men of Concord* until 1935. On October 2, 1934, Greenslet wrote to him to suggest inclusion of the book in Houghton Mifflin's publication list for the fall of 1935. In November 1934 Ira Rich Kent—managing editor at Houghton Mifflin—urged Wyeth to send an outline of his plans for the illustrations. On February 9, 1935, Wyeth wrote to reassure Kent how important the book was to him but, nevertheless, to explain that his work on a triptych altar panel for the National Episcopal Cathedral in Washington would make it difficult for him to meet an autumn deadline. By fall, however, with Houghton Mifflin planning to publish *Men of Concord* in a year's time, Wyeth was ready and able to buckle down. He wrote to Kent on October 12, 1935: "I'm all steamed up about this Thoreau series and the pictures for the book are taking very definite shape in my mind. My recent stay in Concord and my wanderings over Thoreau's haunts again have brought things to a head."[14]

From that point, Wyeth worked energetically on *Men of Concord.* Between October 1935 and the summer of 1936, his letters to Kent, Greenslet, and Lovell Thompson (an editor and later executive at Houghton Mifflin) show growing excitement. They overflow with details of format, book and jacket design, layout, paper, type, illustration placement, and printing. On November 20, 1935, he reported to Kent, "The work is started and the first picture is compelling, I think."[15] On June 21, 1936, he wrote to Greenslet, "The Thoreau series is proving to be the most gratifying job I have done in years and I hope the results will measure up to your expectations."[16] By July he was completing the final picture for the book, putting the last pen-and-ink drawings in the mail, and preparing to drive completed panels to Boston. He wrote to Thompson on July 9, 1936: "There is more heart in this series for *Men of Concord,* and better sustained than [for] any book I ever did. It is [with] real regret that I must conclude the set now."[17]

Men of Concord appeared in November 1936. Wyeth was "deeply pleased" with it.[18] He wrote to Greenslet on November 24, "The splendid books came in to-day and I can enthusiastically say that I am delighted with the way they are gotten up."[19] Wyeth had achieved his long-held ambition to pay homage to Thoreau in an illustrative series. Although the final product varied from his original conception of it eighteen years before, it represented a fulfillment. Response to the book was favorable and sales were good, but his satisfaction derived far more from Thoreau's significance to him than from critical or commercial success.

The book was just off the press when Wyeth began to consider the disposition of the *Men of Concord* panels. He hoped the paintings would remain together, in Concord, preferably in the library. But selling the series as a whole proved impossible. A local historian and library committee member, Allen French, arranged for the display of all the panels in the Concord Free Public Library's new gallery late in 1938. Although Wyeth did not live to see it, the generosity of two Concord families ensured that some of the panels would ultimately hang in the library's Thoreau Room, thus honoring the artist's wish for a series that had so occupied his inner life.

NOTES

Page 22: Andrew Wyeth, *Haying*, ink on paper, The Andrew and Betsy Wyeth Collection.

1. N. C. Wyeth (NCW) to Francis Allen, January 25, 1919, Francis H. Allen Papers, Thoreau Society Collections, Henley Library, Thoreau Institute, Lincoln, Mass.

2. NCW to Julia Starkey, December 14, 1918, N. C. Wyeth/Houghton Mifflin Correspondence, Houghton Mifflin Company Correspondence and Records, MS Am 1925 (1962), Houghton Library, Harvard University, Cambridge, Mass. (hereafter cited as HL).

3. Ibid.

4. NCW to Stimson Wyeth, October 1, 1911, *The Wyeths: The Letters of N. C. Wyeth, 1901–1945*, ed. Betsy James Wyeth (Boston: Gambit, 1971), 389.

5. Julia Starkey to Roger Scaife, memorandum, December 18, 1918, HL.

6. NCW to Roger Scaife, December 22, 1918, HL.

7. Ibid.

8. Roger Scaife to NCW, December 27, 1918, HL.

9. NCW to Francis Allen, January 25, 1919, Allen Papers, Thoreau Society Collections, Thoreau Institute.

10. NCW to Roger Scaife, November 1, 1927, HL.

11. Roger Scaife to NCW, November 3, 1927, HL.

12. Francis Allen to Ferris Greenslet, memorandum, December 3, 1930, HL.

13. Ibid.

14. NCW to Ira Kent, October 12, 1935, HL.

15. NCW to Ira Kent, November 20, 1935, HL.

16. NCW to Ferris Greenslet, June 21, 1936, HL.

17. NCW to Lovell Thompson, July 9, 1936, HL.

18. NCW to Ferris Greenslet, November 24, 1936, HL.

19. Ibid.

“The work is started and the first picture is compelling.”

N. C. WYETH | 1935

THE PAINTINGS by N. C. WYETH

Introduction to the

MEN of CONCORD PAINTINGS

CHRISTINE B. PODMANICZKY

For the *Men of Concord* commission, Wyeth chose to work in what was to him a new method of painting. After decades of using oil pigments on stretched canvas, he executed the *Men of Concord* paintings in oil on Renaissance Panels, hardboard supports of pressed wood commercially sold by the F. Weber Company of Philadelphia. The panels were finished with eight coats of gesso, "each of a special and individual consistency, separately seasoned and rubbed down"; their backs were sealed with a deep maroon-colored paint.[1] They appealed mostly to the egg tempera painters of the period, and Wyeth's son-in-law Peter Hurd, who introduced egg tempera painting to both N. C. Wyeth and Andrew Wyeth in the mid-1930s, probably called them to Wyeth's attention. Wyeth considered the use of oil paint on the wood panels "the most permanent and most luminous method known."[2] The gessoed surface was smooth and provided little resistance to the brush.

Wyeth found that by spreading his paint thinly on these panels, he could create passages in which the clear white of the gessoed ground became part of the design. He could also form highlights by gouging into the ground with a sharp point. Both techniques imparted a luminescence and clarity to the paintings that Wyeth deemed suitable for the spirit of the book. He preferred a matte surface and did not varnish the finished paintings. The overall effect had, Wyeth thought, "a little of the Currier and Ives quality," thus attributing to his illustrations a vision of the American past that in the social upheavals of the 1920s and 1930s seemed "authentic, uncomplicated and pure."[3]

Too many times in his career Wyeth felt that his paintings had suffered in reproduction owing to the limitations of the printing process or careless plate preparation. His letters to Houghton Mifflin show he was extremely concerned—indeed, "scared to death"—by the usual four-color process, which involved multiple plates and press passes per image. He felt the appeal of his new materials and techniques could "spell success for the sale of the book" and that the "ordinary kind [of plates] will lose 75 percent of the particular quality" he achieved in his work.[4] It was crucial to find a process that would retain his artistry. The editors agreed, and *Men of Concord* was printed by a process in which the four-color images were produced in one press pass, reducing the possibility of haziness that was due to poor plate alignment and paper shrinkage. The process also allowed both text and images to be printed on the same paper stock, giving a coherence to the book that is lost when illustrations are printed on paper of different weight and finish.[5]

"The splendid books came in to-day," wrote Wyeth to Houghton Mifflin's director, Ferris Greenslet, in November 1936, noting, "The color work radiates a singularly old fashioned, charming and appropriate appeal." He added, "What a relief to see the color printing on the same letter press paper! . . . How clean and clear are the white passages in the designs!" His only regret—"How I yearned to illustrate *Men of Concord* more extensively!" By the end of the holiday season, Houghton Mifflin had sold approximately four thousand copies at $4.50 each, "not bad for a book of its price in these times."[6]

Correspondence establishes that from the very outset of the commission, Wyeth had intended to sell the paintings as a group. Ten were shown at the Munson-Williams-Proctor Institute in Utica, New York, in March 1938, and another group was shown at the Concord Free Public Library in December 1938. Wyeth hoped to sell them to an individual or institution with Concord associations, but various schemes fell through. By October 1939 he began to offer them singly or in groups.[7] At least eight remained in the artist's estate and were sold after his death by his wife or, later, by his daughter Carolyn.

NOTES

1. The description is quoted from the label that was applied to the backs of the panels.

2. NCW to Paul F. Klaasesz, October 27, 1939. This and all subsequent letter citations are in the Wyeth Family Archives, Chadds Ford, Pa., unless otherwise noted.

3. "A little," NCW to Ferris Greenslet, November 24, 1936, MS Am 1925 (1962), Houghton Library, Harvard University (hereafter cited as HL); "authentic," Hazel Brandenberg, "Re-Presenting the Past: Currier and Ives in 1920s America," *Imprint* (American Historical Print Society, Spring 2012), and quoted by Chris Lane, antiqueprintsblog.blogspot.com/2012/08/e-presenting-past-currierives.html.

4. NCW to Lovell Thompson, February 12, 1936, HL.

5. Conversation, Podmaniczky with Will McGrorty, Pemcor LLC, June 19, 2015.

6. "Splendid book," NCW to Ferris Greenslet, November 24, 1936, HL; "How I yearned," NCW to Dr. Herbert Thoms, January 18, 1937; "not bad," Ferris Greenslet to NCW, December 28, 1936, HL

7. NCW to Eugene Kraetzer, January 30, 1939 (private collection), indicates that Wyeth still hoped to place the paintings in Concord. NCW to Paul F. Klaasesz, October 27, 1939, in which Wyeth offered the Buffalo businessman his choice of any of the paintings except the endpaper illustration, for individual prices ranging from $350 to $800.

MEN of CONCORD

COVER ILLUSTRATION

Oil on hardboard, 38¾ x 32 inches (98.4 x 81.3 cm)
Brandywine River Museum of Art
Gift of Amanda K. Berls, 1980

Wyeth designed this image to capture the attention of a prospective reader. Using techniques he had learned from Howard Pyle and perfected decades earlier, he masterfully draws the reader into the discussion and thus into the book itself. By making two of the Concordians look directly at the viewer, the artist has engaged the viewer/reader in the conversation. Before the reader has opened the book, Wyeth has conveyed an inclusionary tone born of his own conviction that Thoreau's writings were "pertinent . . . profound" and of "practical value to the world."[1]

This scene is the only one of the commission that is not based on a journal entry, and only two of the figures can be identified with any certainty. A young Thoreau, in brown jacket and black tie, looks directly at the viewer; Ralph Waldo Emerson stands next to him, wearing a tall hat. The doorway is suggestive of Concord's architectural heritage, but it doesn't seem to have been drawn from a specific source.

NOTES

1. "Pertinent, profound," NCW, "Thoreau, His Critics and the Public," *Thoreau Society Bulletin* 37 (October 1951), n.p.; "practical value," undated draft of a letter to Christian Brinton, found in NCW's copy of Samuel Arthur Jones, *Thoreau: A Glimpse* (Concord, Mass.: Albert Lane, The Erudite Press, 1903), Brandywine River Museum of Art (hereafter cited as BRMA), N. C. Wyeth House and Studio Collection.

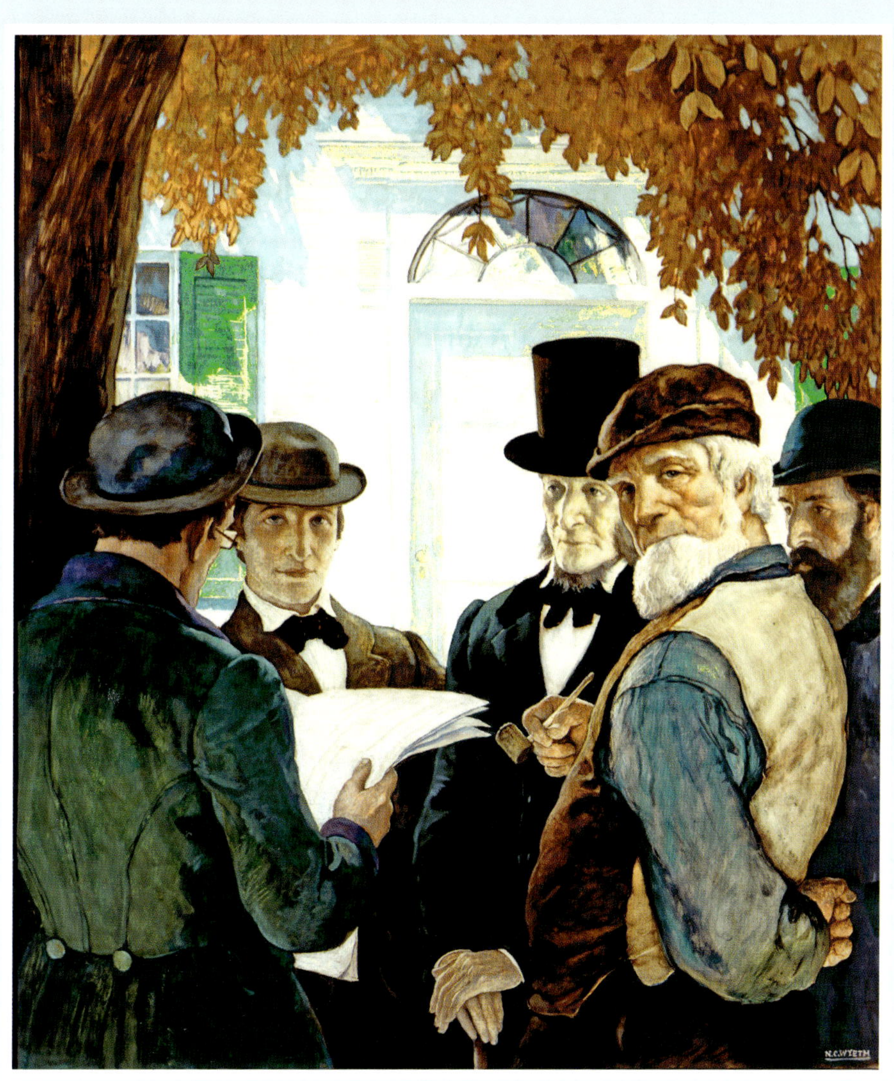
N.C.WYETH

"A man of a certain probity and worth, immortal and natural"

Oil on hardboard, 36 x 32 inches (91.4 x 81.3 cm)
Private collection

For this scene Wyeth found inspiration in *A Winter Sunset,* one of the many photogravures by Herbert W. Gleason that decorate his set of Thoreau's writings. With artistic license, Wyeth removed a line of trees in the middle ground of Gleason's view to better delineate the figure and the ox team. And drawing on decades of creating magnificent skyscapes, he added color to the sky, thus enriching both Gleason's black-and-white picture and Thoreau's description of a New England winter sunset: "Ah, what isles those western clouds! In what a sea!"[1]

Reproduced as the book's frontispiece, the painting was captioned with an abbreviated quote from Thoreau's Journal entry. Thoreau described Cyrus Hubbard as "a man of a certain *New England* probity and worth," a modifier to which Wyeth ascribed as much importance as Thoreau did.[2] Francis Allen underscored Wyeth's New England heritage in his introduction to *Men of Concord.* Wyeth scrawled "New England" on the reverse of this panel, suggesting the scene for him evoked the essential character not just of Concord, but of the entire region.

Although not listed in the brochure, this painting was shown at the Macbeth Gallery in New York City in December 1939, evidence that Wyeth judged it able to stand without textual reference.[3]

NOTES

1. *The Writings of Henry David Thoreau in Twenty Volumes*, Manuscript Edition (no. 281) (Boston: Houghton Mifflin, 1906) (cited hereafter as *The Writings*), BRMA, N. C. Wyeth House and Studio Collection; *A Winter Sunset*, vol. 10, after p. 430; quote, p. 430.

2. Henry David Thoreau, *Men of Concord* (Boston: Houghton Mifflin, 1936), 157.

3. "The Clan Wyeth Presents Its Famed Patriarch," *Art Digest* 14, no. 6 (December 15, 1939).

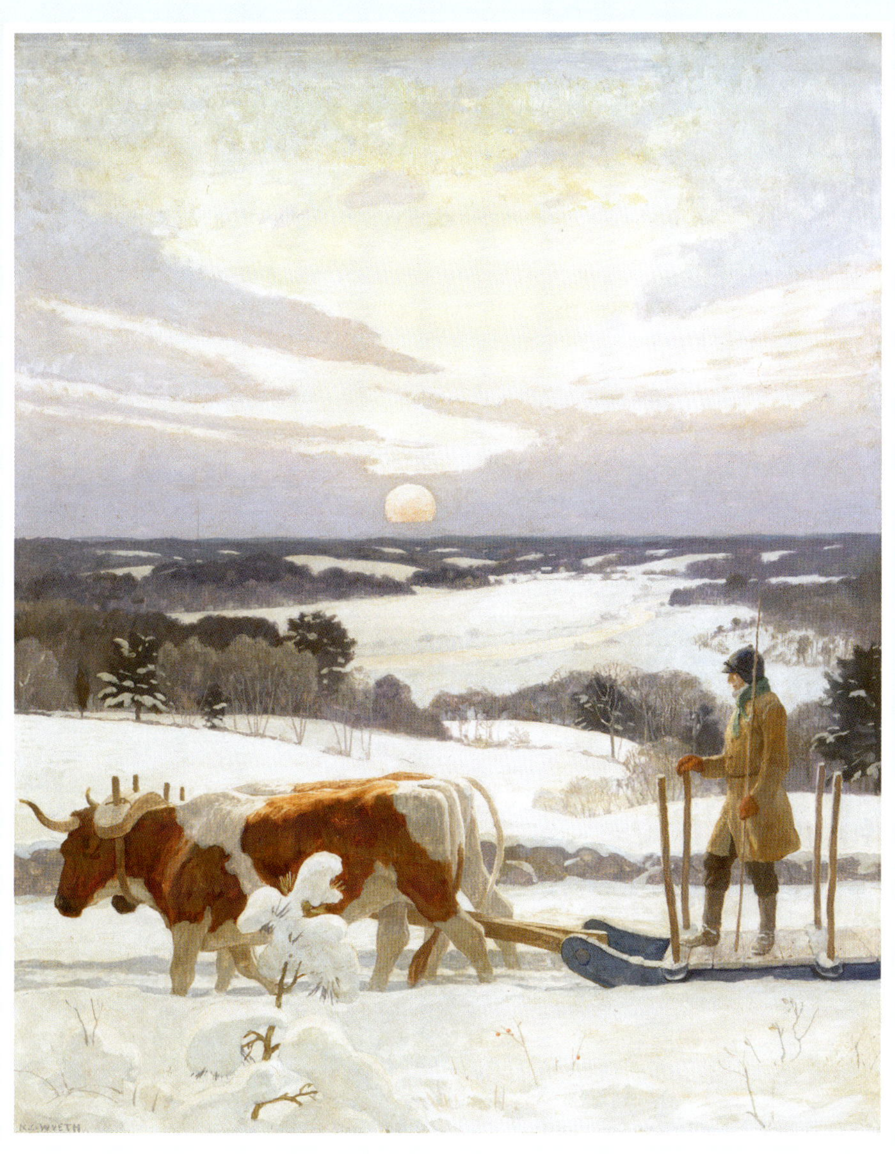
N.C.WYETH

THOREAU FISHING

Oil on hardboard, 38½ x 33 inches (97.8 x 83.8 cm)
Private collection

Fishing was certainly part of Wyeth's boyhood. Later, when Thoreau's writings became important to him, in homage he must have fished at Walden and in the Concord River, which enabled him to impart to the image a valued autobiographical reference. The common experience gave Wyeth one more way to picture Thoreau as an accessible and sympathetic figure, here seen from the perspective of an ambler along the riverbank.

Another of Gleason's photogravures probably served as a primary pictorial reference for this painting. In Wyeth's set of *The Writings, Among the Reeds by the River Low* was flagged with a paper marker (volume 5, after page 395). The visual interest in this black-and-white view of a shoreline thick with reeds and lily pads derives from the interplay of linear and ovoid shapes. Wyeth adopted a similar treatment of the water surface, stretching the pattern to almost meet the reflection of trees on the opposite bank.

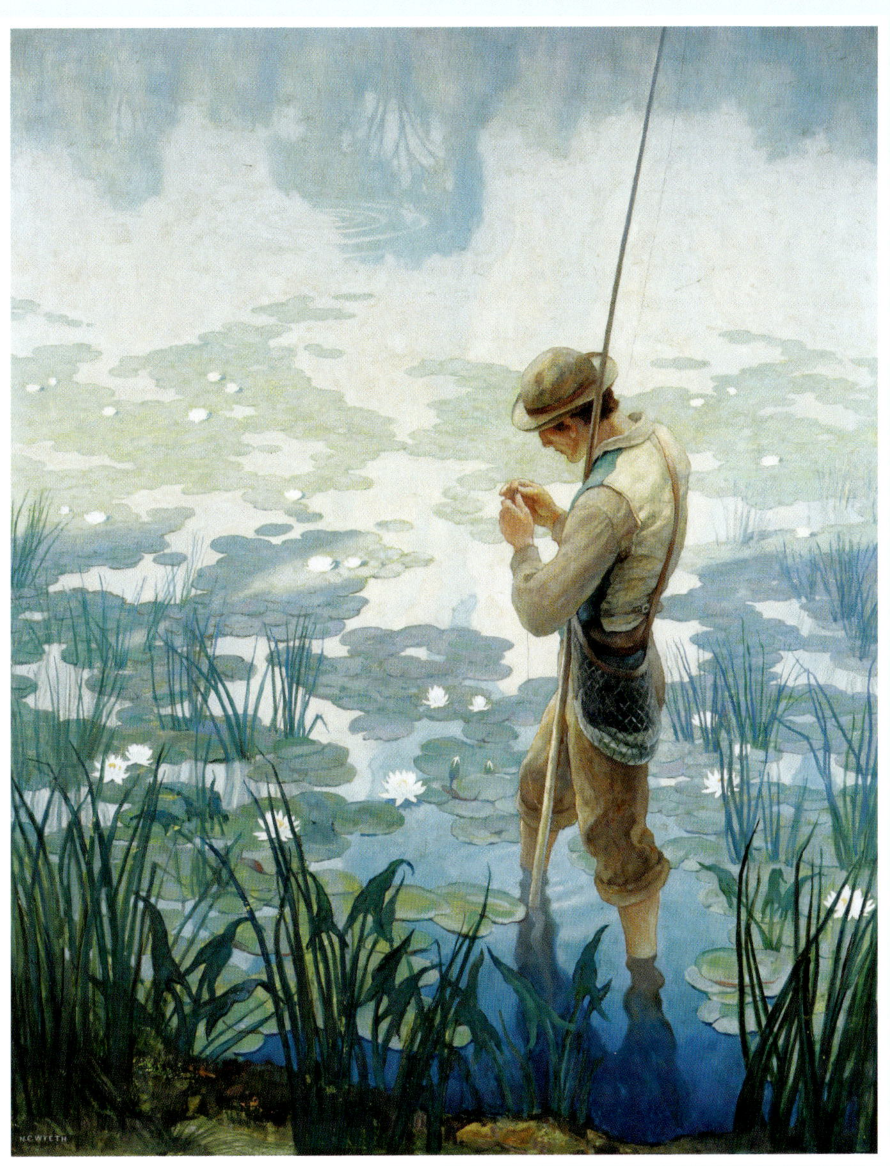
N.C.WYETH

THE CARPENTERS REPAIRING HUBBARD'S BRIDGE

Oil on hardboard, 38¾ x 28¾ inches (98.4 x 73.0 cm)
Presented to the Concord Free Public Library by
Mr. and Mrs. Caleb Henry Wheeler in memory of Caleb Kendall Wheeler, 1947
Courtesy William Munroe Special Collections
Concord Free Public Library Corporation

N. C. Wyeth's appreciation of Concord's Revolutionary War history certainly preceded his interest in the town's literary heritage, and his earliest historical illustration (*The Minute Man,* published in the *Delineator,* October 1905) depicts the rabble of minutemen at the famous bridge. Although the excerpt from Thoreau's Journal quoted in *Men of Concord* specifically refers to Hubbard's Bridge, a bridge over the Sudbury River, it seems likely that Wyeth used as his resource Gleason's photogravure of the North Bridge across the Concord River, titled *The First Battle-ground of the Revolution* (volume 1, after page 14).

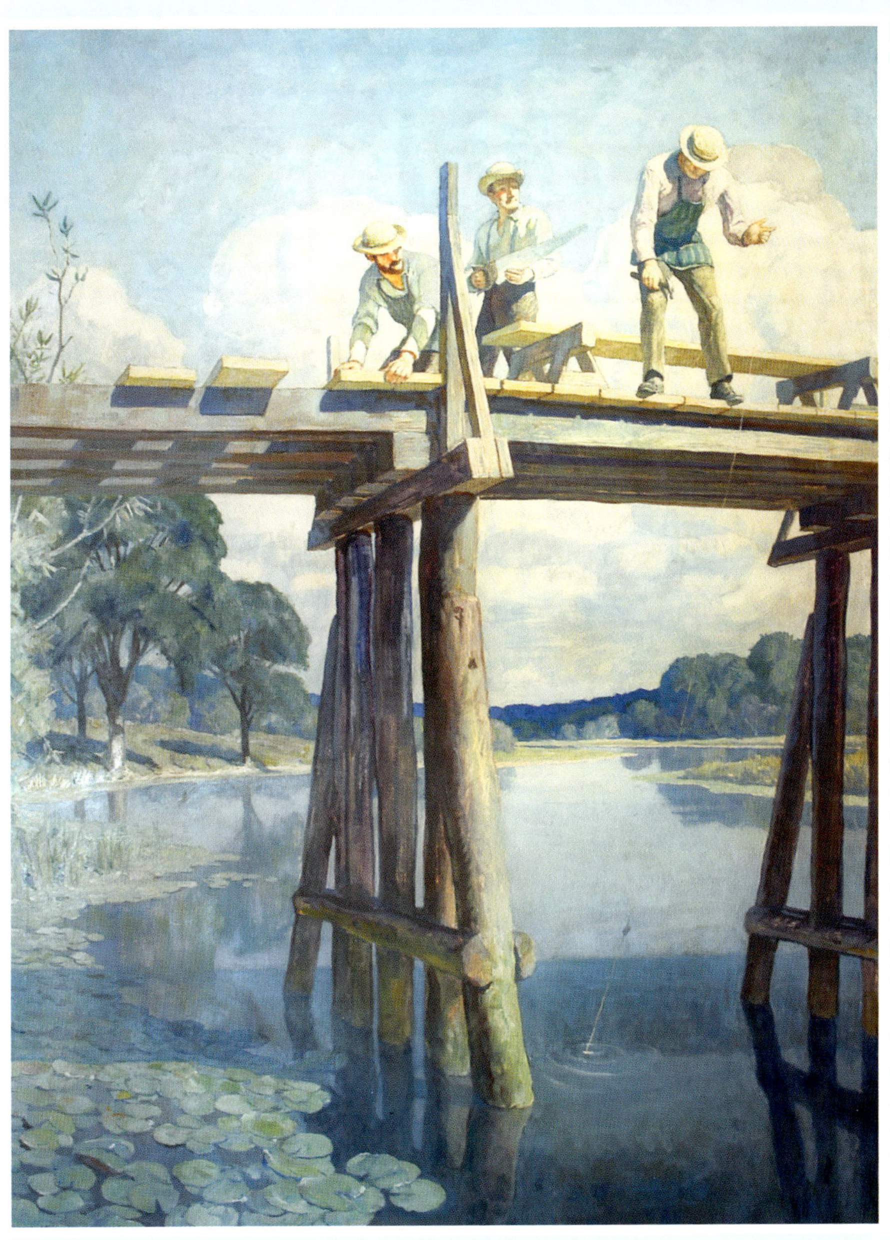

THOREAU and MISS MARY EMERSON

Oil on hardboard, 37¾ x 28¾ (95.9 x 73.0 cm)
Purchased by the Concord Free Public Library from the Samuel Hoar Fund, 1947
Courtesy William Munroe Special Collections
Concord Free Public Library Corporation

In the illustrations that depict Thoreau, Wyeth tried to discredit prevailing notions that Thoreau was an uncouth and unsociable woodsman. Here Wyeth placed him in the company of Ralph Waldo Emerson's aunt Mary Moody Emerson (1774–1863). A great thinker and journalist herself, Emerson was, by Thoreau's own account, "a genius, as woman seldom is, reminding [him] less often of her sex than any woman" he knew. Interestingly, Wyeth generally subscribed to Thoreau's opinions and rarely ceded intellectual parity to women he met.

In November 1935 Wyeth wrote to Ira Rich Kent of Houghton Mifflin to request a pictorial reference for Mary Moody Emerson. Kent responded that the only known source was a silhouette published in *The Writings*. In his own set of *The Writings,* Wyeth scrawled "Mary Emerson?" next to the passage that reads, "One a sedate, indefatigable knitter, not spinster, of the old school, who had the supreme felicity to be born in days that tried men's souls," thus appropriating a textual reference in Thoreau's journal for Mary Emerson's knitting.[1]

The contents of Ralph Waldo Emerson's study were installed in a re-creation of the room in the new Concord Museum across the street from the Emerson House in 1930, both of which Wyeth may have visited. For his immediate reference, however, Wyeth drew the table and lamp after those shown in a postcard view of Emerson's study that he kept in his studio.[2]

NOTES

1. *The Writings*, 7:31.
2. BRMA, Collection of the Walter and Leonore Annenberg Research Center

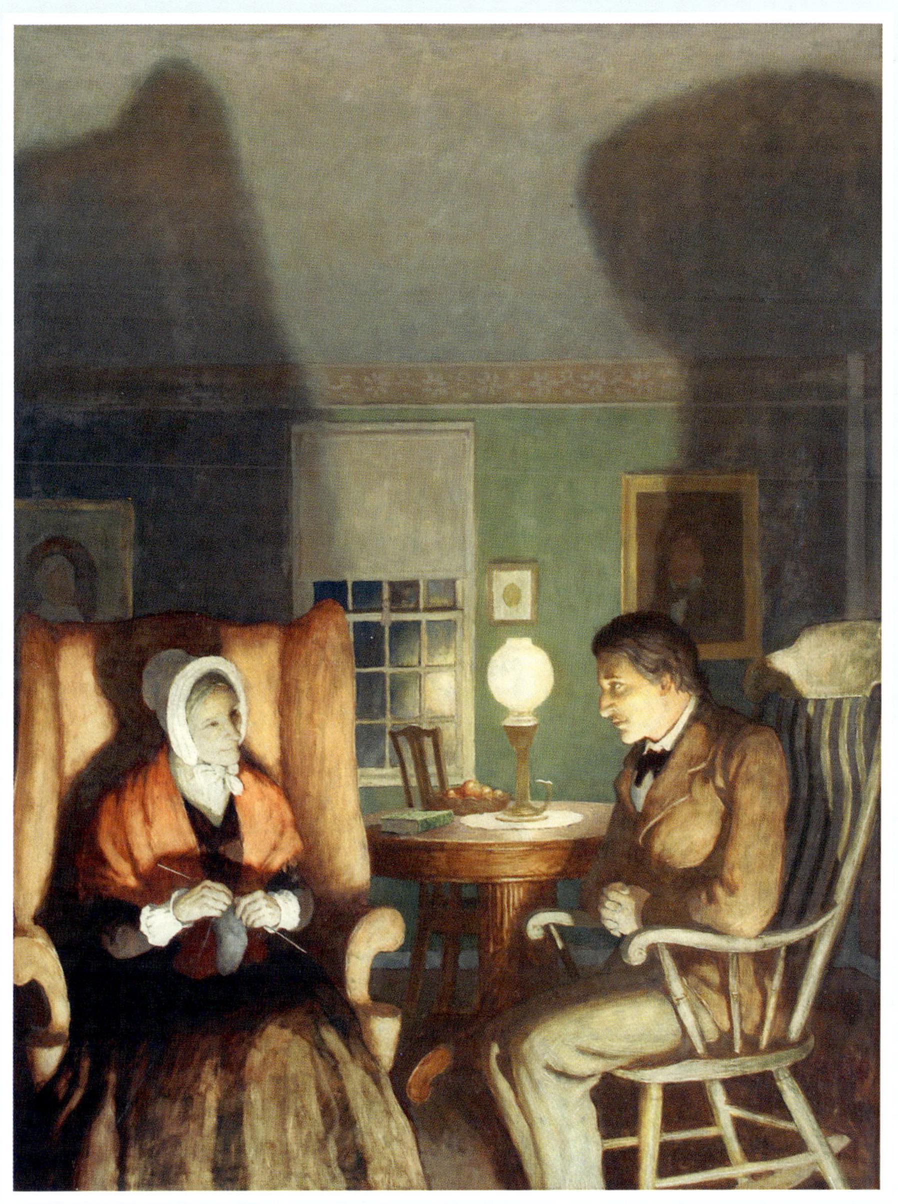

MR. ALCOTT in the GRANARY BURYING GROUND in BOSTON

Oil on hardboard, 43⅛ x 32 inches (109.5 x 81.3 cm)
Boston Athenaeum

Wyeth had access to many printed images of the Granary Burying Ground, including a postcard view in his collection. The most important visual resource for this painting, however, came from *Curious Old Gravestones in and about Boston,* a portfolio of heliotypes by Howland Shaw Chandler published in 1924. Chandler inscribed a copy to Wyeth that same year.[1] Plate 23 in that volume depicts the 1697 gravestone of Ruth Carter, which Wyeth copied almost exactly in the painting's foreground, including the two skeletons on the stone, described as "remarkably fine examples of the stone-cutter's art." Wyeth took his view of the cemetery from a slightly different angle than Chandler had, but he retained in the upper left of the composition a glimpse of the iron fence and buildings along Tremont Street that appeared in Chandler's photograph. The record and stone of Dr. John Alcock, Bronson Alcott's ancestor, has disappeared, and though Thoreau noted that Alcott saw it in 1852, N. C. Wyeth probably did not, constructing his own design inspired by photos in the portfolio.[2]

Although Thoreau in his journal entry fondly mocked Alcott for his genealogical research, Wyeth placed great importance on family history and occasionally used the experiences of his forebears as a rationale for his ability to sympathetically illustrate particular stories or narratives. In the case of *Men of Concord,* he felt his New England heritage was central to his interpretations.

NOTES

1. Walter Rowlands, *Curious Old Gravestones in and about Boston,* photographed by Howland Shaw Chandler (Boston: n.p., 1924), BRMA, N. C. Wyeth Studio Collection. NCW's copy, inscribed by Howland Chandler, is dated "Aug. 4, 1924." Plate 23 is the only plate of fifty with tack holes at the top, suggesting the sheet was hung for study.

2. City of Boston, Historic Burying Grounds Initiative, www.cityofboston.gov/Parks/HBGI/search.asp.

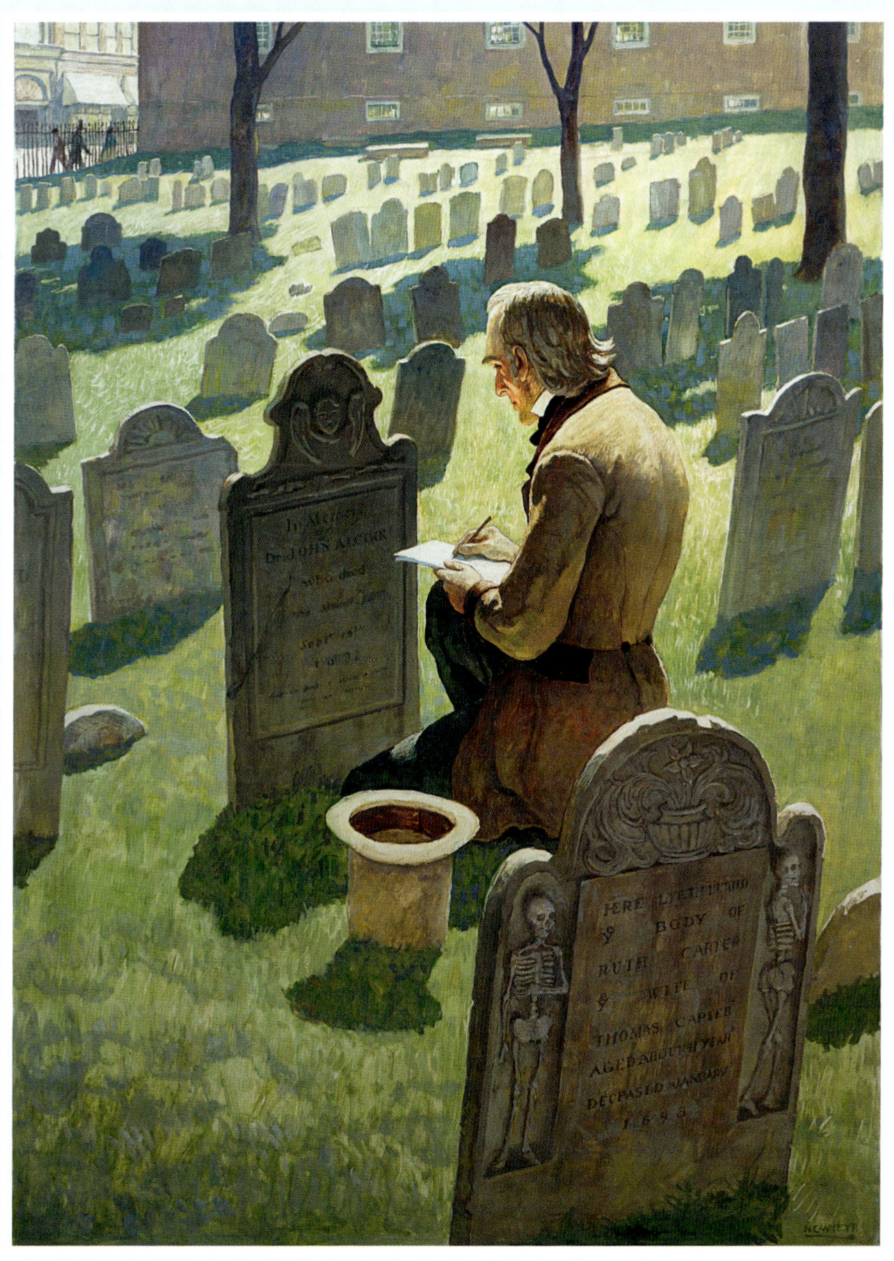
Dr. JOHN ALCOCK
BODY OF
RUTH
THOMAS
DECEASED

THOREAU and the THREE REFORMERS

Oil on hardboard, 43 x 32 inches (109.2 x 81.3 cm)
Private collection

Wyeth achieved a sense of authenticity in this picture with an attention to detail that makes his illustrations so enjoyable to examine. From the tea service and lusterware sugar bowl to the footed compote on the sideboard set against the lively pattern on the wall, the painting is filled with delightful, historically accurate details. The engraving hanging above the sideboard is recognizable as Washington Allston's *Saul and the Witch of Endor,* issued by the American Art Union in 1852, a copy of which hung in N. C. Wyeth's studio.[1] The print illustrates a biblical scene in which the spirit of Samuel warns Saul that the Philistines will conquer his people. Both Thoreau and Wyeth would have been familiar with the use of the word Philistine to describe someone antagonistic to artistic or poetic culture.

Thoreau named the "three reformers" in his Journal entry and described their characters as "slimy," each ready to take the starch out of his clothes. Wyeth's decision to let the viewer/reader imagine Thoreau's reaction for himself or herself reflects Wyeth's conception of how an illustration should function.

NOTE

1. *Saul and the Witch of Endor,* after Washington Allston, engraved by Charles Edward Wagstaff, circa 1852, BRMA, N. C. Wyeth House and Studio Collection.

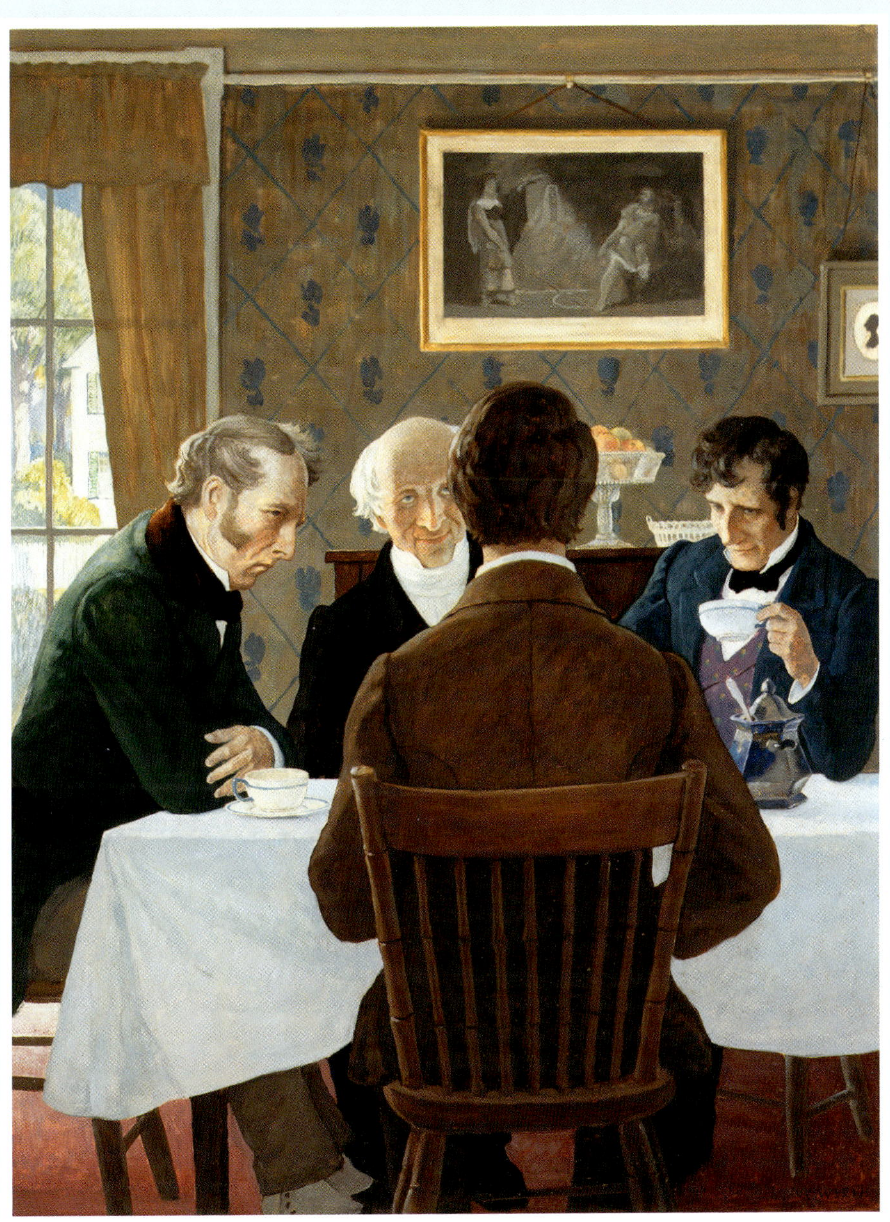

THE MUSKRAT-HUNTERS, GOODWIN and HAYNES

Oil on hardboard, 42½ x 30⅞ inches (107.9 x 78.4 cm)
Displayed in the Concord Free Public Library since 2003 and included in this exhibition in memory of Emilie Norton Thomas by her family.

Wyeth had always felt that an illustrator was free to augment a text, to choose a line or thought that an author had left unworked. But he was careful to note the details specified in a text and employ them where necessary. In his journal entry of October 22, 1853, Thoreau describes John Goodwin as "one-eyed"—and Wyeth accordingly added the eye patch to his depiction of Goodwin.

Again, one of Gleason's photogravures probably served as a visual resource for this image. Wyeth left in his copy of *The Writings* (volume 7, after page 122) a paper marker at a scene of the river flooding its banks, titled with an excerpt from Thoreau's poetry, "The river swelleth more and more, like some sweet influence stealing o'er the passive town."

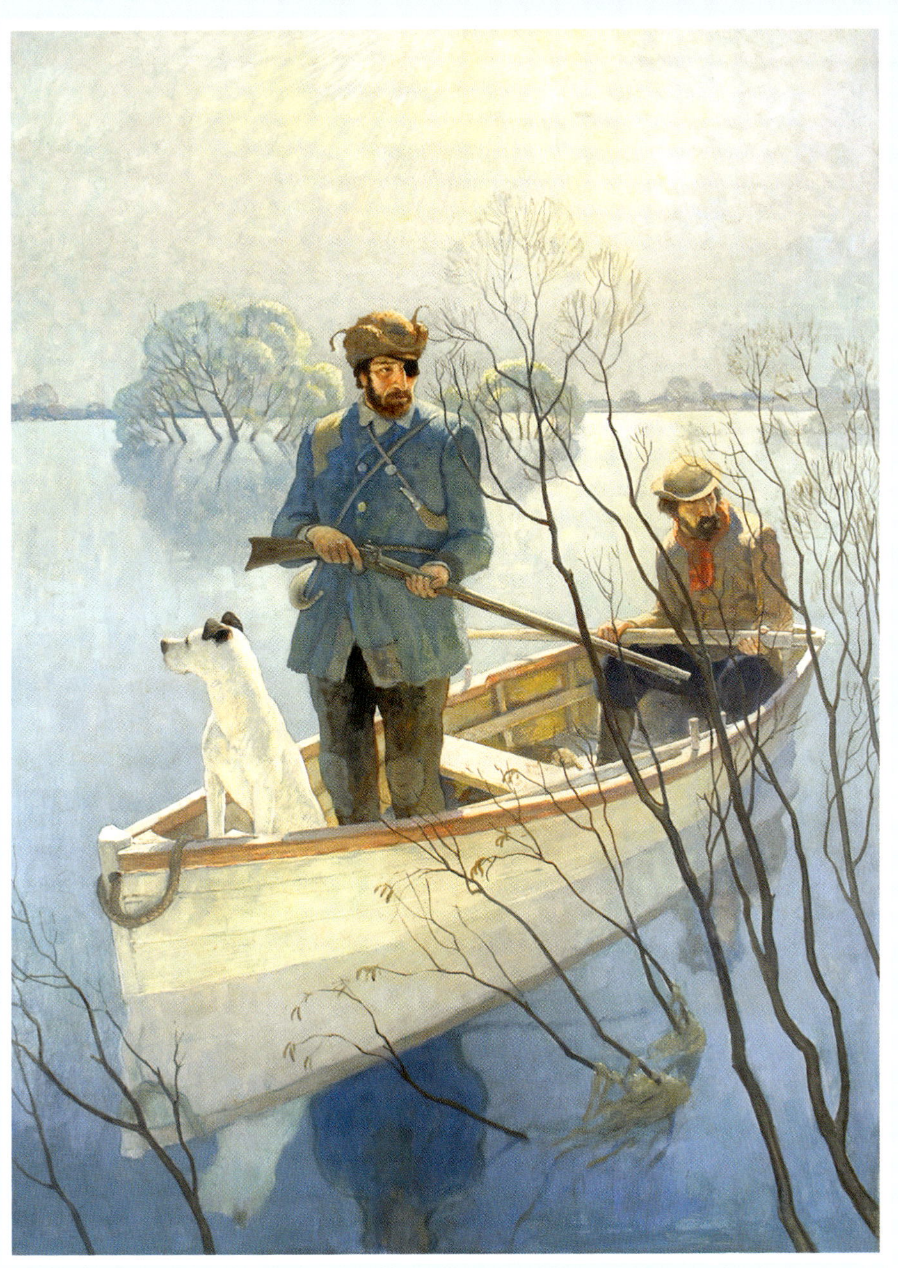

FISHING THROUGH the ICE

Oil on hardboard, 42¼ x 31¼ inches (107.3 x 79.4 cm)
Displayed in the Concord Free Public Library since 2003 and included in this exhibition in memory of Emilie Norton Thomas by her family.

In 1912, clearly under the influence of his first forays into Thoreau's writings, Wyeth wrote to his brother Stimson, "I have lately developed a craving to execute a series of pictures depicting 'Pickerel Fishing through the Ice'. . . my mind has brimmed with our experience as boys on Cushing's Cove." Wyeth urged Stimson to write "a true and intimate story, . . . utilizing all those endeared local details of implements and action." This project was never realized, but as Wyeth considered the subjects of his illustrations in early 1935, he informed Houghton Mifflin's Ira Rich Kent that the series would be "fundamentally autobiographical" and that his own life had included "similar physical activities which make up the background of Thoreau's thinking." Wyeth carefully rendered those memories of ice fishing, perfectly capturing the distinctive shape of pickerel, the simplicity of the tip-ups, and the wintery light from a pale sun seen through a leaden New England sky.[1]

Thoreau's journal entry for December 7, 1856, describes a scene similar to the one Wyeth depicted, but that passage is not included in *Men of Concord.*

NOTE

1. "I have lately," NCW to Stimson Wyeth, January 1, 1912; "fundamentally" and "similar," NCW to Ira Rich Kent, January 6, 1935, MS Am 1925 (1962), Houghton Library, Harvard University.

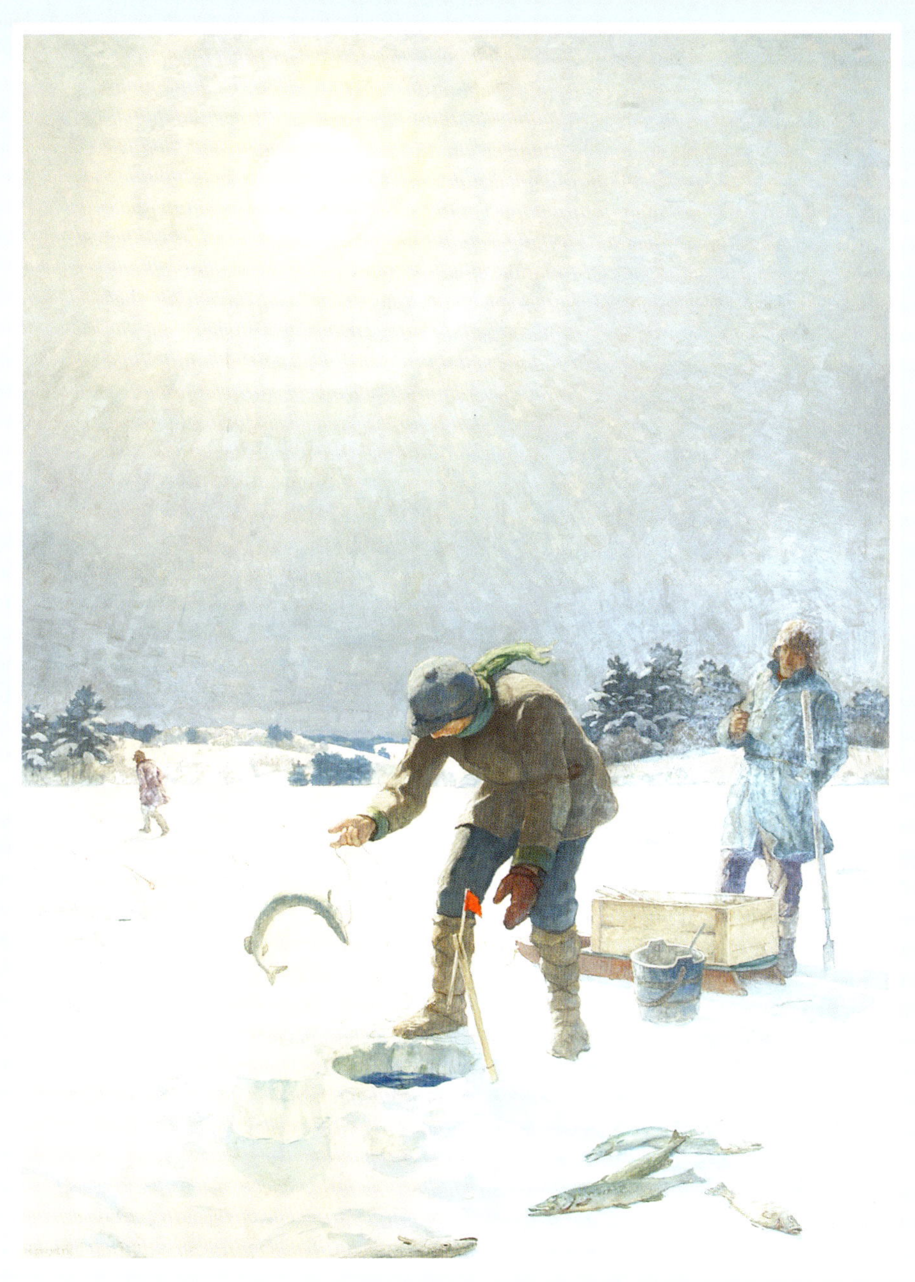

BAREFOOTED BROOKS CLARK BUILDING WALL

Oil on hardboard, 34½ x 28 inches (87.6 x 71.1 cm)
Collection of American Illustrators Gallery, New York

In August 1936 Wyeth wrote to Leslie Greenough of Houghton Mifflin to express his opinion on the caption for this illustration. He was adamant that the proper colloquialism, as written in Thoreau's Journal entry, be used: Building Wall instead of Building *a* Wall. Such verbal tics that spoke to regional distinctions were important to both Thoreau and Wyeth.

Among the Gleason photogravures reproduced in *The Writings,* there are a number of views of stone walls. In this choice of subject matter, however, Wyeth probably paid homage to another New England writer, Robert Frost, whom he considered his "greatest discovery since Thoreau, in the realms of wonderful expression." He first read Frost's *North of Boston* in 1916, which includes the poem "Mending Wall." He admired Frost's "wonderful and exquisite themes" for the rest of his life.[1] Undoubtedly, Wyeth found the stone wall symbolic of aspects of the New England landscape and character; five of the twelve *Men of Concord* paintings include at least a suggestion of a stone wall.

NOTE

1. NCW to HZW, October 9, 1916; NCW's copy of *North of Boston* (New York: Henry Holt, 1914) remains in his studio library, BRMA, N. C. Wyeth House and Studio Collection.

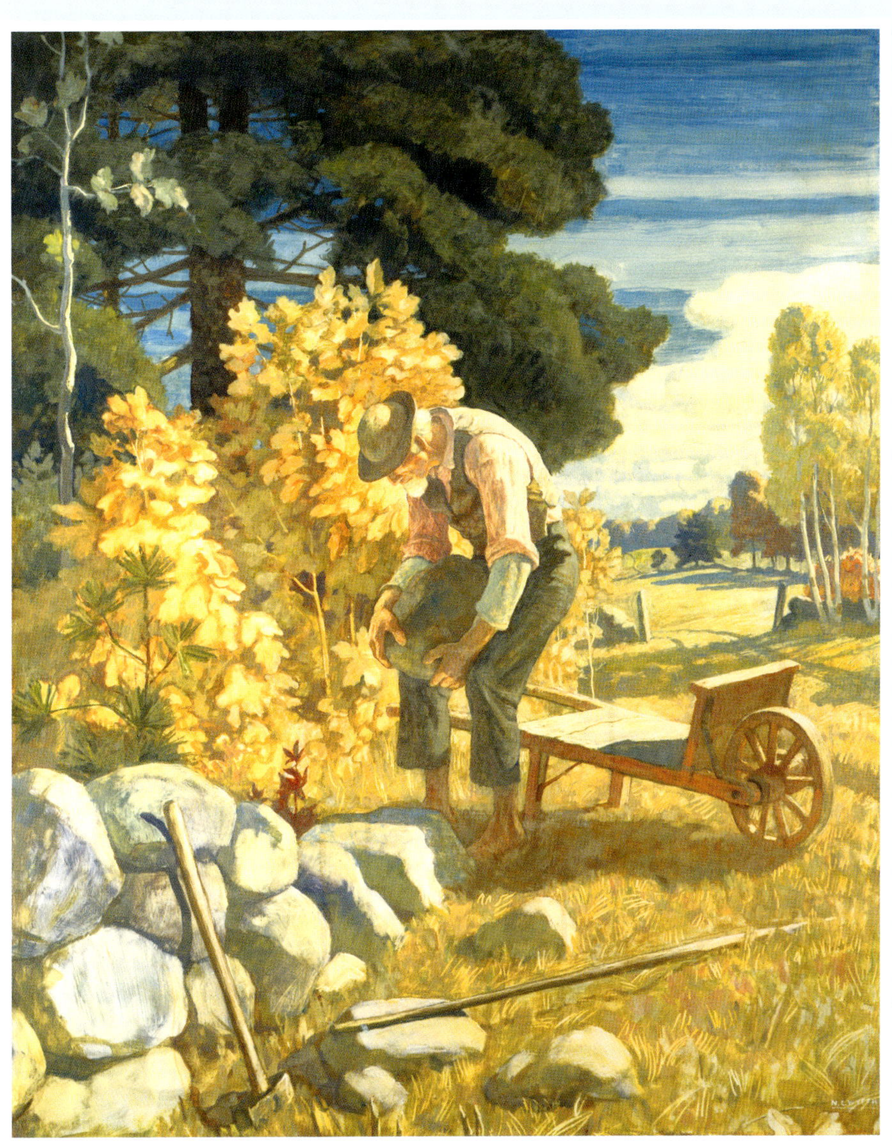

JOHNNY and his WOODCHUCK-SKIN CAP

Oil on hardboard, 37¾ x 28¾ inches (95.9 x 73.0 cm)
Purchased by the Concord Free Public Library from the Samuel Hoar Fund, 1947
Courtesy William Munroe Special Collections
Concord Free Public Library Corporation

Wyeth's teacher, Howard Pyle, urged students in his illustration classes to acquire artifacts related to their areas of concentration; Pyle himself had an impressive collection of eighteenth-century American decorative arts and costumes to support his interest in colonial and post-Revolutionary narratives. Pyle recognized that these objects, when studied closely, could reveal stories and information omitted in formal histories, material that could prove valuable to an illustrator. So instructed, Wyeth first collected Western artifacts; then, as his interest in Western subjects subsided, he amassed the everyday objects of country life that were fast becoming obsolete, such as oxen yokes, spinning wheels, butter churns, and country clocks. He continued to acquire a wide variety of props throughout his career.

Wyeth found that he shared with Thoreau a similar interpretation of the power of objects, and he emphasized Thoreau's insight by selecting this passage to illustrate. Johnny's cap "suggested so much of family history," Thoreau wrote, "[the] adventure with the chuck, story told about it, not without exaggeration, the human parents' care of their young these hard times." For Thoreau these stories were integral to the hat; so Wyeth, too, appreciated the stories evoked by objects such as the coonskin cap, colonial cocked hat, and Civil War kepi in his studio collection.[1]

NOTE

1. Thoreau's relationship with the material world is documented by David F. Wood in *An Observant Eye: The Thoreau Collection at the Concord Museum* (Concord, Mass.: Concord Museum, 2006)

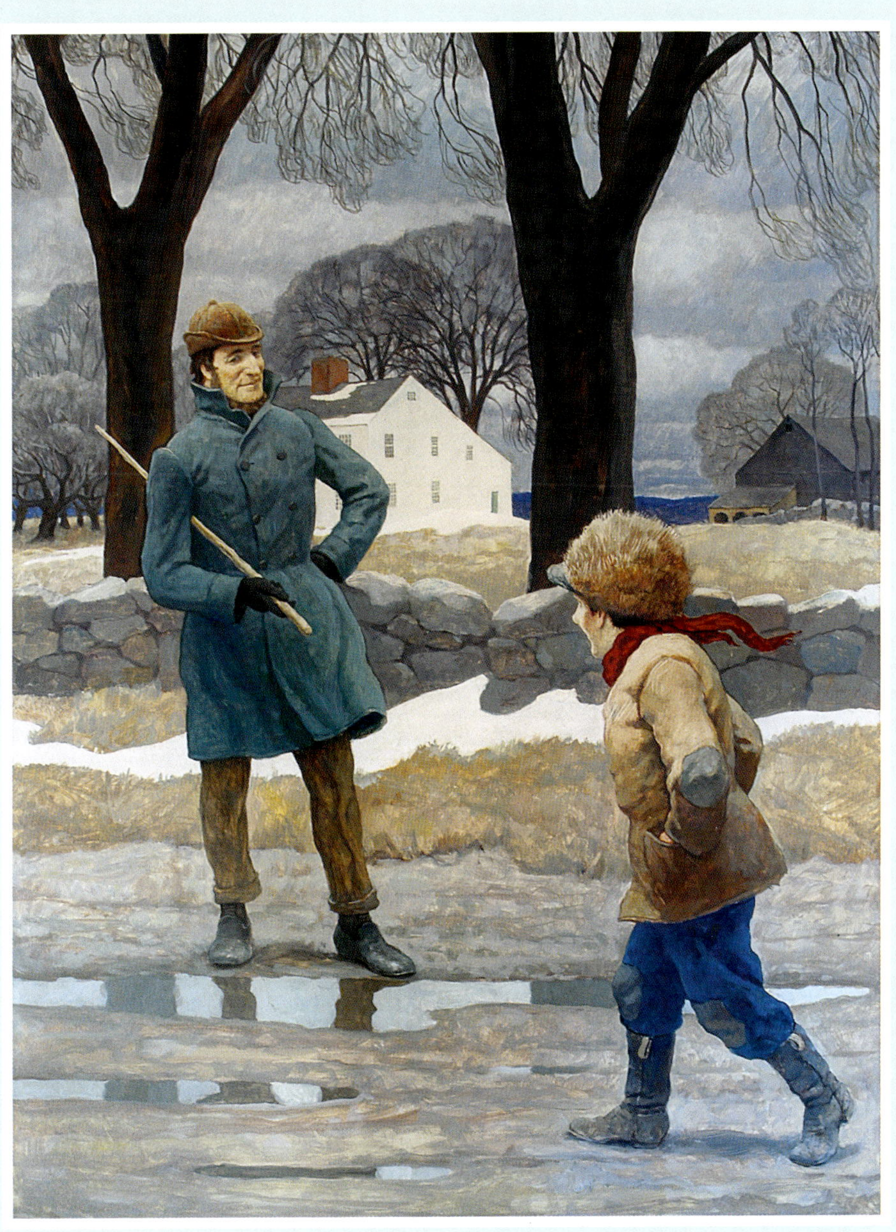

MEN of CONCORD

ENDPAPER ILLUSTRATION

Oil on hardboard, 28⅝ x 41 inches (72.7 x 104.1 cm)
Arkell Museum at Canajoharie,
Gift of Bartlett Arkell, 1940

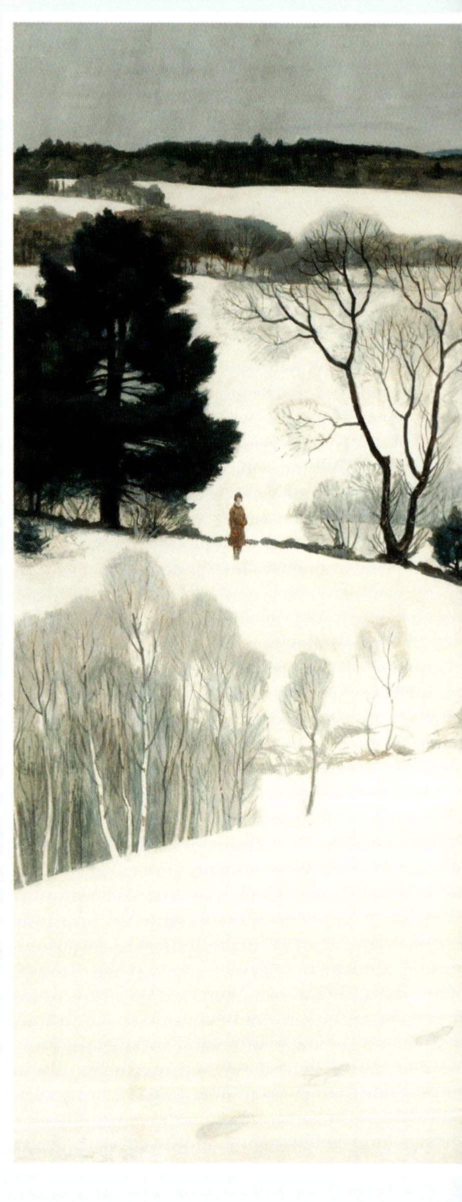

This painting, described by N. C. Wyeth as "unquestionably the most significant" of the series, may be seen as a tribute to Thoreau and Winslow Homer, both men extremely influential in his thinking and art.[1] For Wyeth, both Homer and Thoreau showed their genius by elevating "the little into the great," a phrase he borrowed from William Henry Channing's description of Thoreau as published in Sanborn's *Life of Henry David Thoreau.*[2] Wyeth would have known well Winslow Homer's *Fox Hunt* (1893), which had hung at the Pennsylvania Academy of the Fine Arts since 1894.

Wyeth may have drawn initial inspiration for the scene from Thoreau's Journal entry of January 30, 1841, a lyrical passage in which Thoreau described his sighting of a fox in a winter landscape. The artist used one of Gleason's photogravures as his primary visual resource for the landscape. *Winter Landscape from Fairhaven Hill* (volume 7, after page 296) was found flagged with a paper marker in Wyeth's copy of the volume. The artist stepped back from Gleason's view and simplified the details before adding the distant figure of Thoreau and the fox. Wyeth considered this painting more than a book illustration, and he included it, as *Fox in the Snow,* in his first solo exhibition in New York, held at the Macbeth Gallery in December 1939.

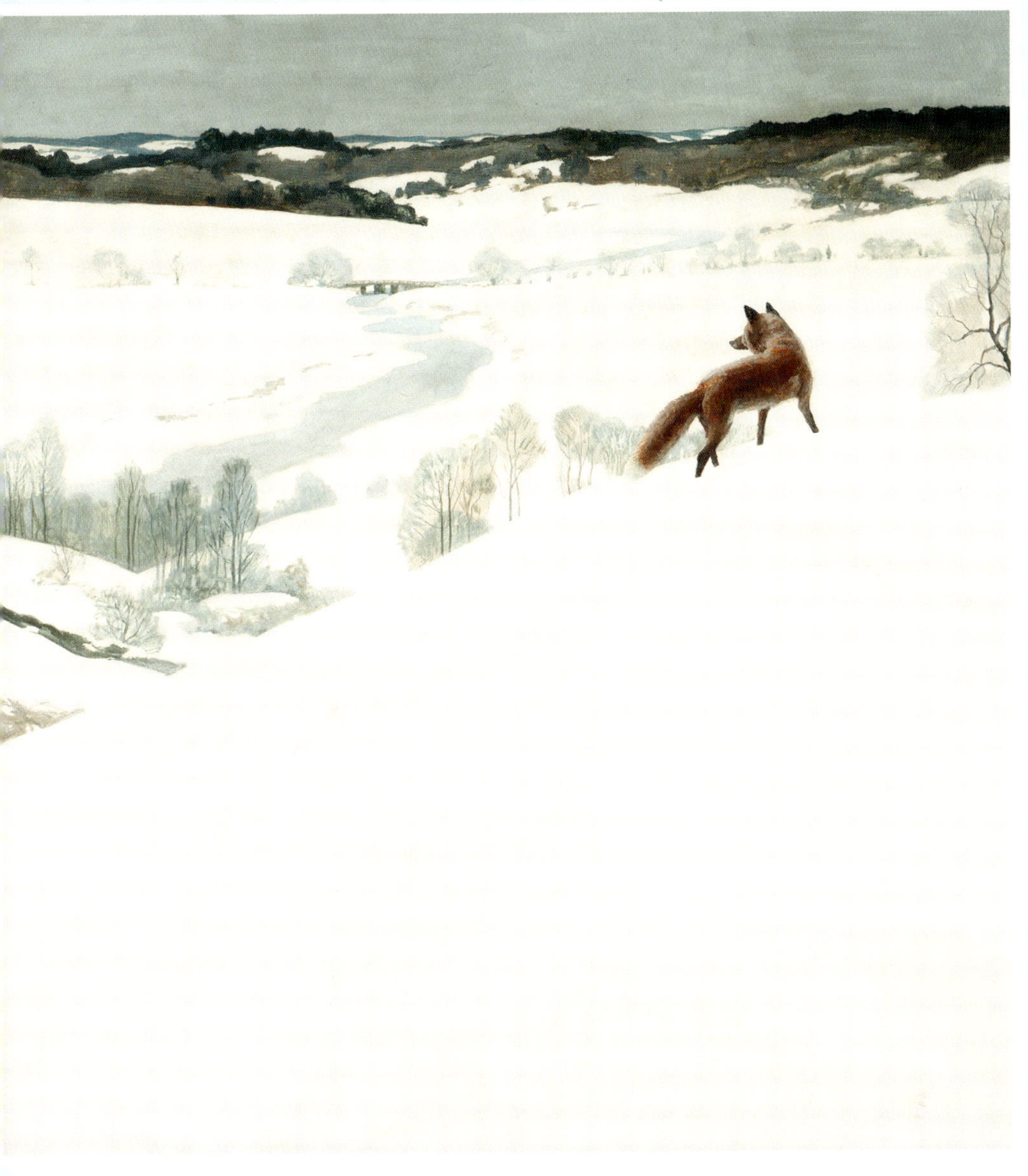

NOTES

1. NCW to Ruth Robinson Wheeler, May 3, 1945, as quoted in Leslie Perrin Wilson, "N. C. Wyeth, Thoreau, and Men of Concord," *Concord Saunterer,* n.s., 8 (2000): 83.

2. The phrase is quoted from William Ellery Channing's *Thoreau, the Poet-Naturalist, with Memorial Verses* (Boston: Charles Goodspeed, 1902), which Wyeth acquired in 1912.

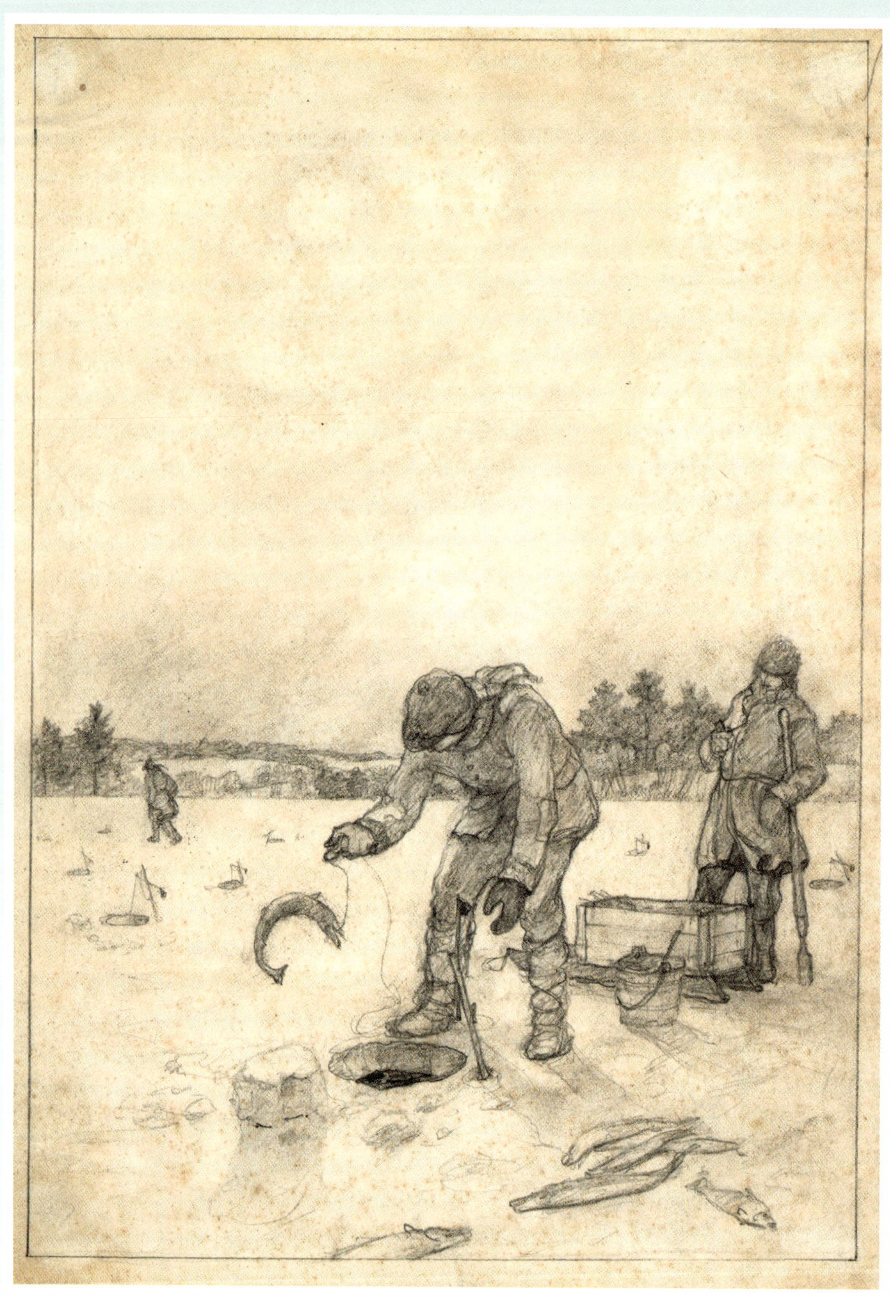

Fishing Through the Ice

N. C. WYETH | COMPOSITION DRAWING | 1936

Graphite on paper, 17⅛ x 12⅛ inches (43.5 x 30.8 cm)
The Andrew and Betsy Wyeth Collection

THE DRAWINGS and OTHER WORKS

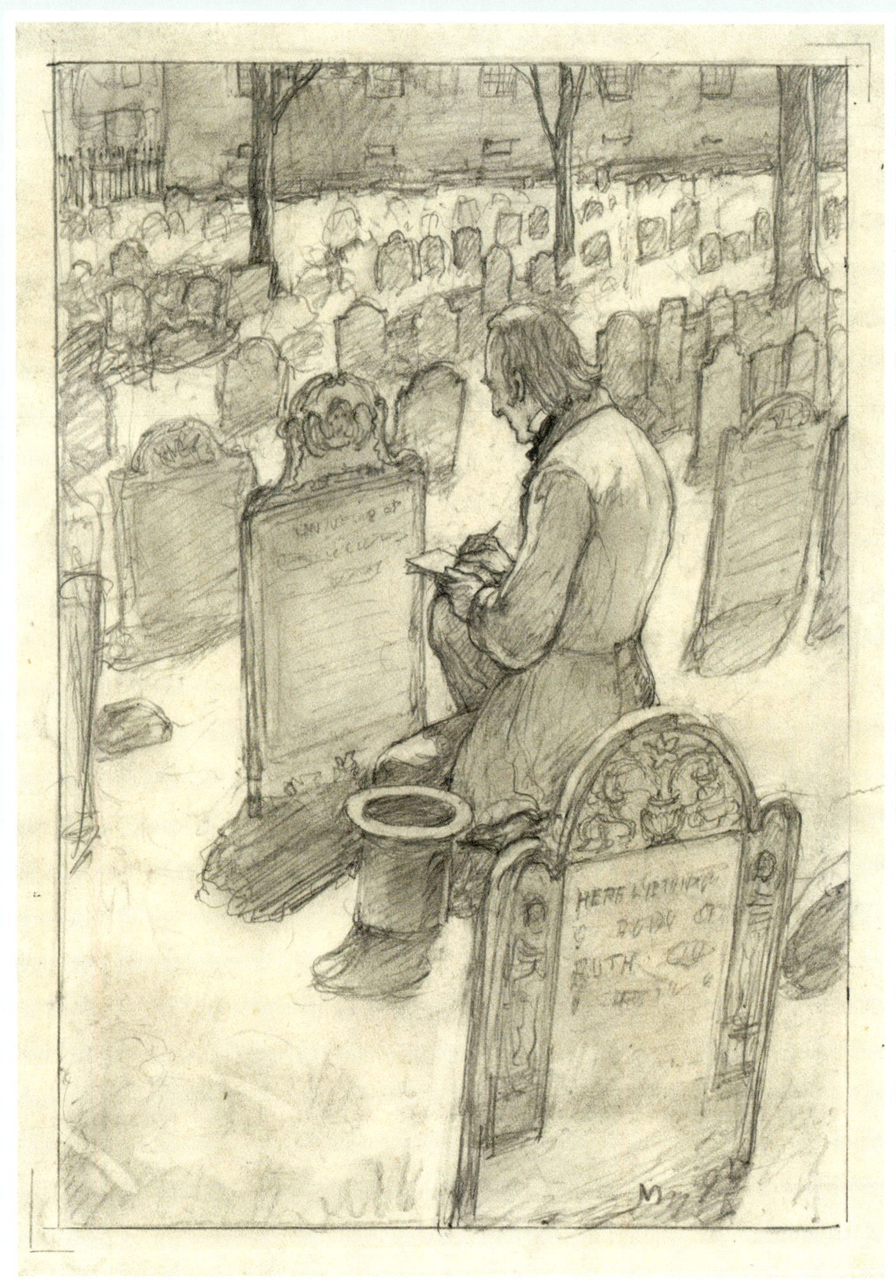

Mr. Alcott in the Granary Burying Ground in Boston

N. C. WYETH | COMPOSITION DRAWING | 1936

Graphite on paper, 13 x 9 inches (33.0 x 22.9 cm)
The Andrew and Betsy Wyeth Collection

Wyeth constructed the *Men of Concord* paintings in a manner that was relatively new to him. For decades he had roughed out his compositions directly onto canvas, with or without the aid of preparatory sketches. For this series he made a detailed composition drawing on paper in pencil or charcoal for each painting. The drawings were sent to a commercial photography studio where a 4 x 3¼-inch (10 x 8.3 cm) lantern slide of each drawing was made. Using a slide projector, he then projected the slides onto the Renaissance Panels to transfer the designs from paper to painting supports. The drawings had little commercial value in Wyeth's day and the artist often gave them away as gifts. To date, only nine of the twelve composition drawings have been located, but lantern slides for all were found in the artist's studio.

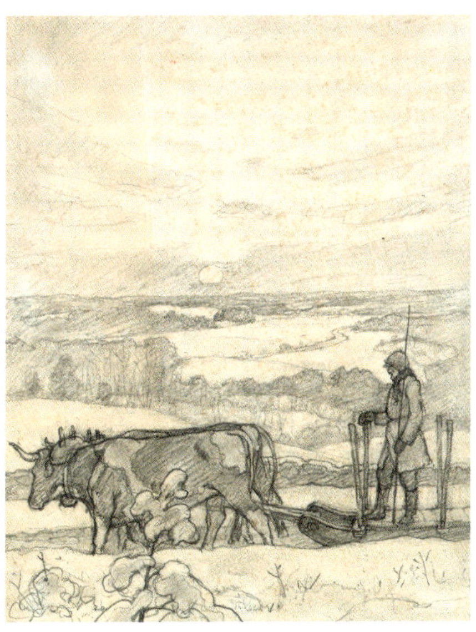

"A man of a certain probity and worth, immortal and natural"

N. C. WYETH | COMPOSITION DRAWING | 1936

Graphite on paper, 14⁷⁄₁₆ x 11³⁄₈ inches (36.7 x 28.9 cm)

The Andrew and Betsy Wyeth Collection

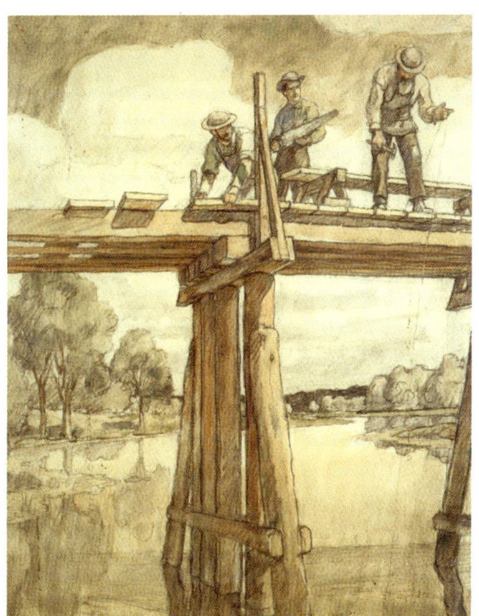

The Carpenters Repairing Hubbard's Bridge

N. C. WYETH | COMPOSITION DRAWING | 1936

Graphite, charcoal, and watercolor on paper, 32⁷⁄₈ x 24³⁄₈ inches (83.5 x 61.9 cm)

Private collection

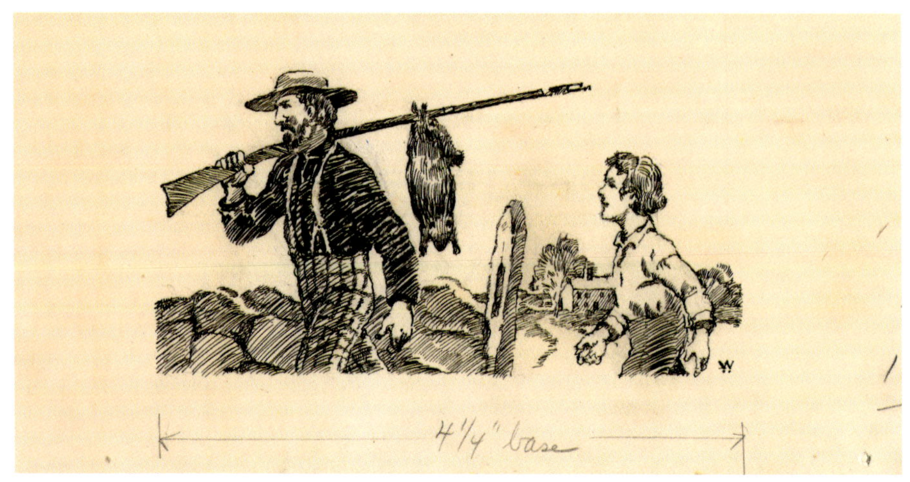

Untitled
(A Woodchuck-Skin Cap)
5 x 9⅞ inches (12.7 x 25.1 cm)

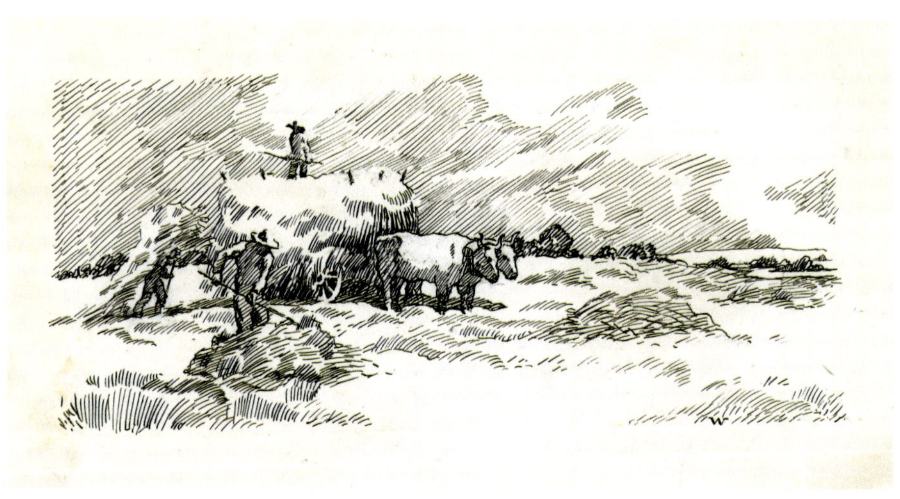

Untitled
(Haying)
9¼ x 12½ inches (23.5 x 31.8 cm)

EIGHT DRAWINGS for MEN of CONCORD, 1936

ANDREW WYETH (1917–2009)

Ink on paper, sheet sizes vary. The Andrew and Betsy Wyeth Collection

---

Twenty-four line drawings decorate the pages of *Men of Concord,* lending an old-fashioned charm to the appearance of the book and evoking the less accomplished line drawings that occasionally occur in the pages of Thoreau's writings. N. C. Wyeth's pen-and-ink work was first published in Scribner's Magazine in 1908; for major books such as *The Mysterious Island* (1918), *The Courtship of Miles Standish* (1920), *Rip van Winkle* (1921), and *Drums* (1928), he contributed head- and tailpieces in ink. But pen and ink was not Wyeth's preferred medium—the original drawings for *Rip Van Winkle,* for example, show many places where the artist scratched away the surface of the paper to correct his strokes. In fact, he wrote to Houghton Mifflin's Roger L. Scaife that he would never be "a good pen man."[1] By 1936, then, Wyeth considered himself lucky to have a son who, at the age of nineteen, had already demonstrated a remarkable facility with the pen. Unbeknown to Wyeth's editors at Houghton Mifflin, the pen drawings that illustrated *Men of Concord*—many signed with an ambiguous "W"—were done by Andrew Wyeth. Even in Andrew's copy of *Men of Concord,* N. C. masked the debt he owed his son, writing, "To Andy on Nov. 23, With many, many thanks for his contributions to this volume—Pop!" The family secret emerged only in 1973, when Douglas Allen Jr. credited the pen drawings to Andrew Wyeth in his book *N. C. Wyeth: The Collected Paintings, Illustrations and Murals.*[2]

NOTES

1. NCW to Roger L. Scaife, July 6, 1920, Houghton Library, Harvard University.

2. Andrew Wyeth's copy of *Men of Concord* remains in the Wyeth Family Archives. Douglas Allen and Douglas Allen Jr., *N. C. Wyeth: The Collected Paintings, Illustrations and Murals* (New York: Crown Publishers, 1972), 220. Douglas Allen Jr. and Andrew Wyeth did not discuss the attribution until 2008, when Wyeth confirmed the drawings as his work. Conversation, Podmaniczky with Douglas Allen, July 8, 2015.

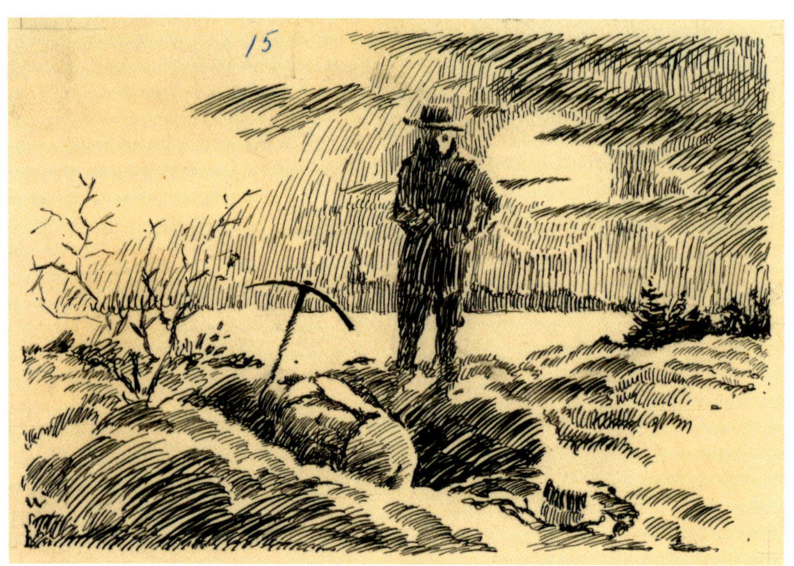

Untitled
(Pirate Money)
3¼ x 4⅝ inches (8.3 x 11.7 cm)

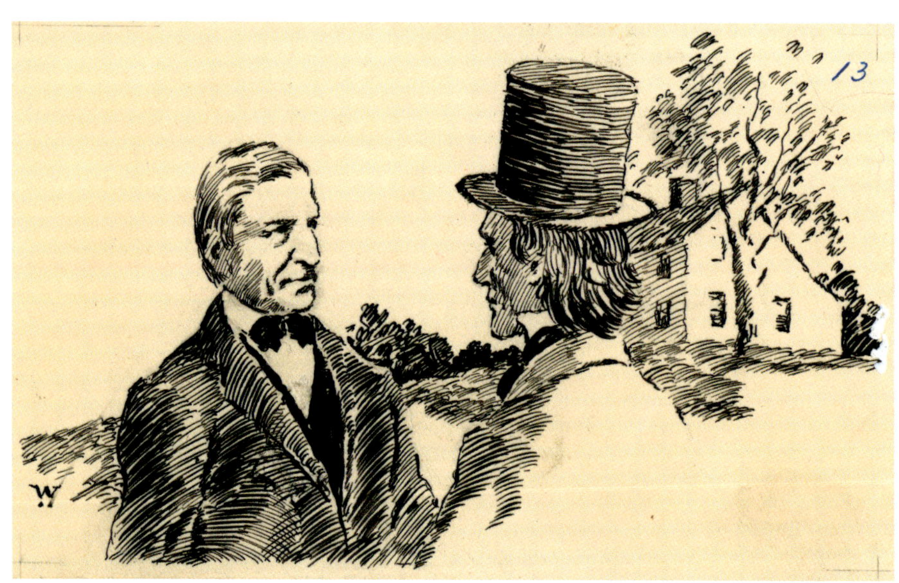

Untitled
(Emerson and Alcott)
3⅛ x 4⅞ inches (7.9 x 12.4 cm)

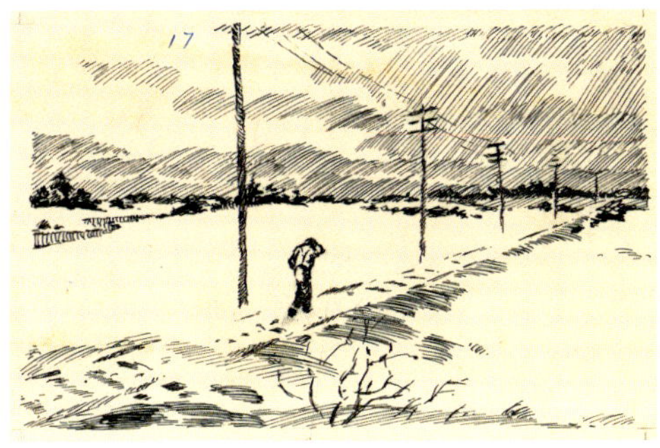

Untitled
(Little Johnny Riordan)
3¼ x 5 inches (8.3 x 12.7 cm)

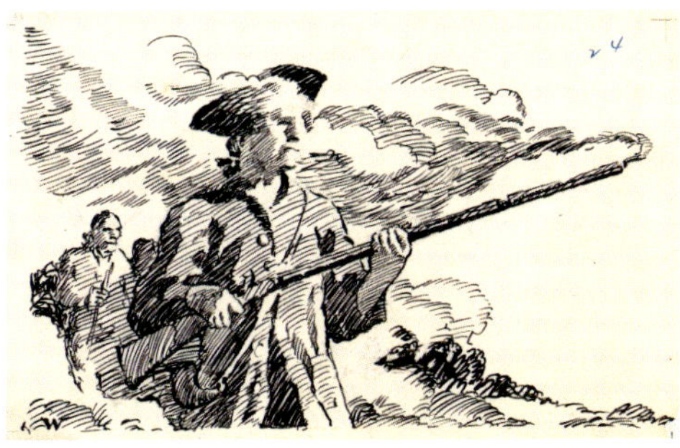

Untitled
(A Farmer of Sentiment)
3⅛ x 4⅞ inches (7.9 x 12.4 cm)

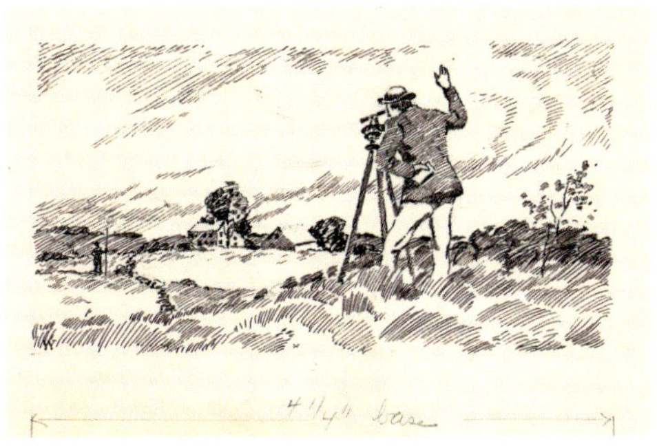

Untitled
(Companions in Surveying)
6 x 9⅛ inches (15.2 x 23.2 cm)

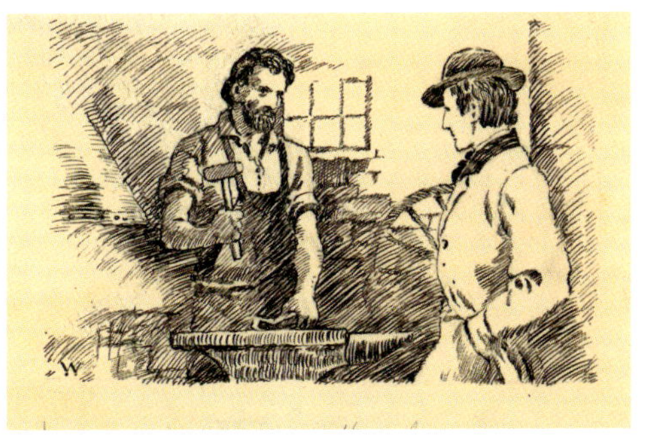

Untitled
(A Talk with the Blacksmith)
4¼ x 9½ inches (10.8 x 24.1 cm)

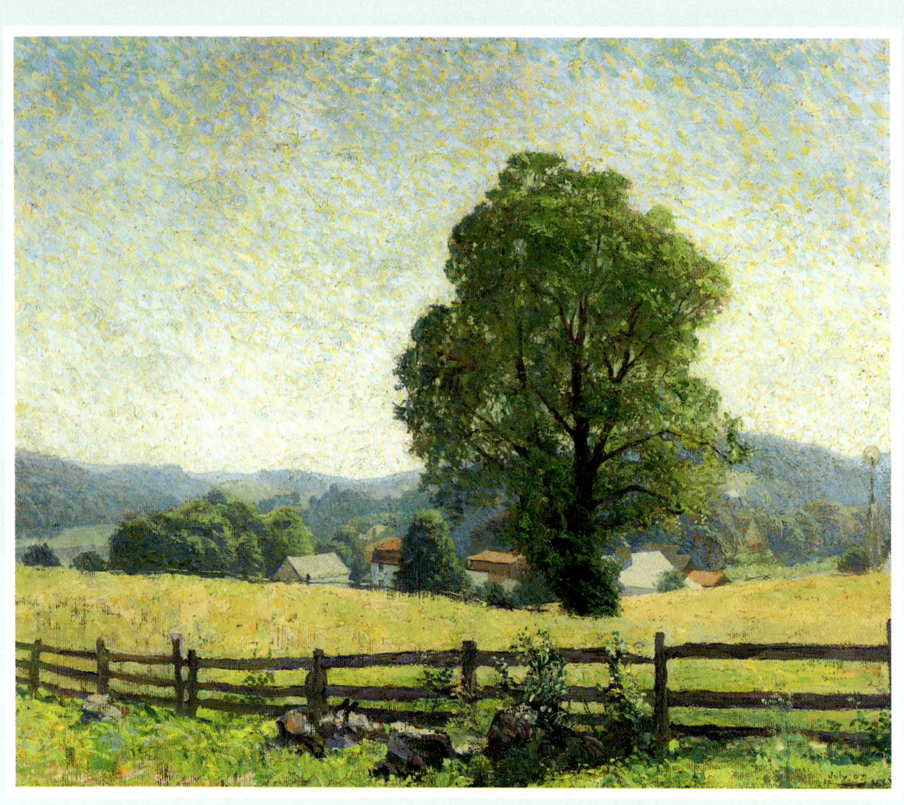

CHADDS FORD LANDSCAPE – JULY 1909

N. C. WYETH | 1909

Oil on canvas, 25 x 30¼ inches (63.5 x 76.8 cm)
Brandywine River Museum of Art
Gift of Mr. and Mrs. Andrew Wyeth, 1970

Wyeth's early attempts to paint under the influence of Thoreau's nature writings resulted in a group of landscape paintings in impressionist styles, all done within steps of or a short walk from Wyeth's studio. "And so it is that I am beginning to realize," Wyeth wrote, "that there are just as big things around one's very threshold as can be found anywhere—it is only for one to find them out." This painting depicts the view to the village of Chadds Ford as seen from the converted carriage house that Wyeth used as a studio in 1909. Wyeth, eloquent in words as well as in paint, wrote: "As I look out of the window into the blaze of the noon heat, everything looks faded and gray, as though all the life and color of the tree-foliage and grass had withdrawn itself from the scorching sun. And with the vanished color has gone the life-blood of the leaves for they rustle like paper and shiver and tremble in the hot breeze. I have started a small canvas embodying this spirit of noon-day."[1]

NOTE

1. NCW to HZW, July 30, 1909.

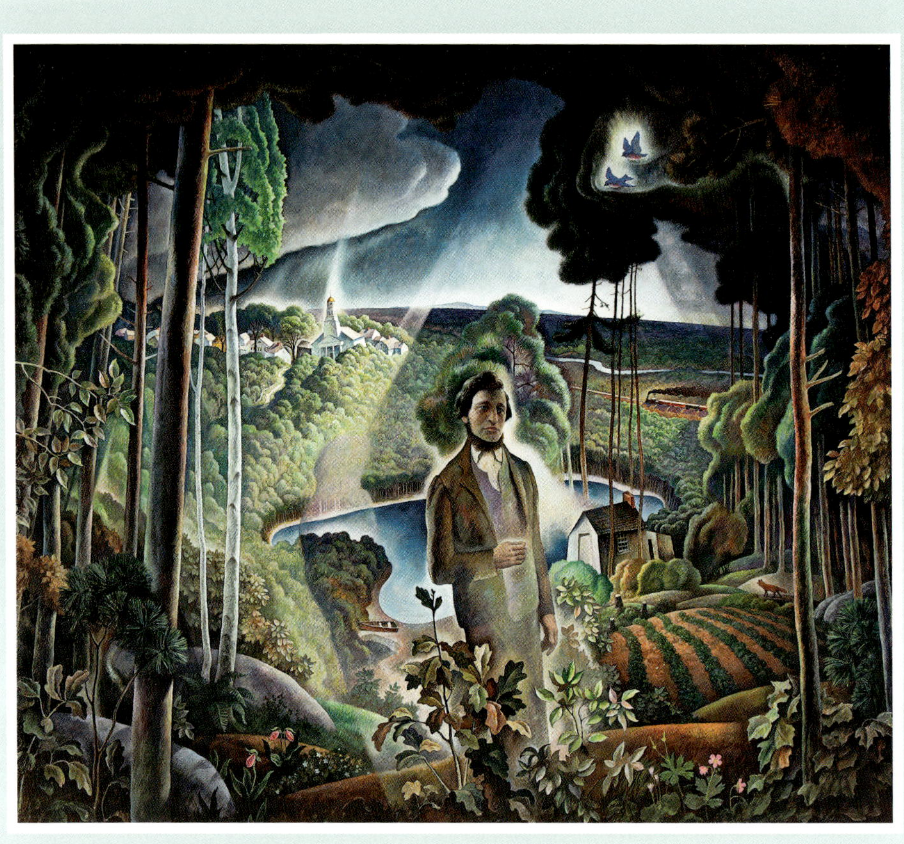

WALDEN POND REVISITED

N. C. WYETH | 1942

Tempera, possibly mixed with other media, on hardboard,
42 x 48 inches (106.6 x 121.9 cm)
Brandywine River Museum of Art, Bequest of Carolyn Wyeth, 1996

Walden Pond Revisited is almost identical to another painting of the same title Wyeth executed in late 1932. The first version, in oil on canvas, is larger (58⅛ x 70 inches; 147.6 x 177.7 cm); the artist exhibited it four times before 1937, and he authorized its use as an advertisement for Henry Seidel Canby's *Thoreau* (Boston: Houghton Mifflin, 1939). The artist first explored tempera painting in 1936 and came to associate the medium with a historical weight and permanence that he felt elevated a subject. Thus, he replicated in tempera several of his earlier, deeply personal canvases, including *Walden Pond Revisited.*

In letters to a Houghton Mifflin editor, Wyeth wrote that the idea for the painting came after spending several nights at Walden Pond. It is encyclopedic in its Thoreauvian imagery: many of the well-known symbols appear—the pond; the one-room hut, bean field, and boat; the fox and bluebirds; the train with its belching smoke; the nearby town of Concord; and, on the horizon, the slight bump of Mount Wachusett. Thoreau looms wraithlike over the scene, his facial features in both versions indistinct, although the source was most likely the crisp Maxham daguerreotype published in *The Writings.* Wyeth treated the facial features of his mother, an equally important figure in his life, in the same manner in a posthumous portrait of 1929.

The carefully rendered botanical portraits in the foreground allude not only to Thoreau's detailed nature writings but also to the Gleason photogravures of botanicals that decorate *The Writings.* Such skyscapes with dramatic shafts of sunlight appear in several Gleason photogravures, particularly *The Frowning Clouds* (volume 1, after page 406). The painting's mixture of realism and fantasy, the strong palette, and the exaggerated forms of clouds and landscape signaled Wyeth's membership in the Regionalist movement. In choosing aspects of contemporary style for the composition, Wyeth underscored his firm belief that Thoreau's writings spoke to the twentieth century.

SUPPORTING MATERIALS from the BRANDYWINE RIVER MUSEUM of ART

FROM THE COLLECTION OF THE BRANDYWINE RIVER MUSEUM OF ART,
N. C. WYETH HOUSE AND STUDIO COLLECTION,
BEQUEST OF CAROLYN WYETH, 1996:

Lantern slides of charcoal drawings for *Men of Concord:*
Mr. Alcott in the Granary Burying Ground in Boston; Fishing Through the Ice;
Thoreau and Miss Mary Emerson

The Writings of Henry David Thoreau in Twenty Volumes, Volume 5.
Boston: Houghton Mifflin, 1906.

The Writings of Henry David Thoreau with Bibliographical Introductions and Full Indexes, Volume II. Walden; or, Life in the Woods. Riverside Edition.
Boston: Houghton Mifflin, 1893.

The Writings of Henry David Thoreau with Bibliographical Introductions and Full Indexes, Volume III. The Maine Woods. Riverside Edition.
Boston: Houghton Mifflin, 1893.

The Writings of Henry David Thoreau with Bibliographical Introductions and Full Indexes, Volume VII. Autumn. Riverside Edition.
Boston: Houghton Mifflin, 1892.

The Writings of Henry David Thoreau with Bibliographical Introductions and Full Indexes, Volume VIII. Winter. Riverside Edition.
Boston: Houghton Mifflin, 1887.

The Writings of Henry David Thoreau with Bibliographical Introductions and Full Indexes, Volume IX. Excursions. Riverside Edition.
Boston: Houghton Mifflin, 1893.

Samuel Arthur Jones. *Thoreau: A Glimpse.* Concord, Mass.: Albert Lane, The Erudite Press, 1903.

FROM THE COLLECTION OF THE WALTER AND LEONORE ANNENBERG RESEARCH CENTER, BRANDYWINE RIVER MUSEUM OF ART:

Francis H. Allen, ed. *Men of Concord, and Some Others, As Portrayed in the Journal of Henry David Thoreau.* Boston: Houghton Mifflin, 1936.

Houghton Mifflin Company. *Books for Gifts, 1936.* Boston: Houghton Mifflin, 1936.

Tear sheets for *Men of Concord:* Endpaper; *Thoreau Fishing* (Noted on verso in NCW's hand: "Thoreau Fishing at Walden Pond"); *Fishing Through the Ice; Barefooted Brooks Clark Building Wall* (Noted on verso in NCW's hand: "New England Wall Builder"); *Johnny and his Woodchuck-Skin Cap* (Noted on verso in NCW's hand: "Henry D. Thoreau—1859 / Concord Mass"); *Thoreau and the Three Reformers*

Postcards (published by Mrs. G. N. Tanner, Concord, Massachusetts) from N. C. Wyeth's "visual reference collection": Old North Bridge; The Home of Emerson (1835–1882); Thoreau's Home at Lake Walden; Emerson's Study; "Old Manse"

ACKNOWLEDGMENTS

CONCORD ADVISORY COMMITTEE

Peggy Burke, *Executive Director, Concord Museum*

Kerry Cronin, *Director, Concord Free Public Library*

O. Mario Favorito, *Vice President, Concord Free Public Library Corporation*

Lisa Foote, *Vice President, Concord Museum*

Sherry Litwack, *President, Concord Free Public Library Corporation*

Leslie Perrin Wilson, *Curator, William Munroe Special Collections, Concord Free Public Library*

David Wood, *Curator, Concord Museum*

And with sincere gratitude to Richard D. Briggs, Jr., *Chair, Board of Trustees, Concord Museum, and Treasurer, Concord Free Public Library Corporation*

The influence of Thoreau's writings on N. C. Wyeth has been noted in past publications, but the upcoming anniversary of Thoreau's birth in 2017 suggested the occasion for a more comprehensive study. Margaret Burke recognized the need, and I extend my thanks to her for the invitation to join the Concord Museum's project. My contribution was greatly enriched by Curator David Wood, who generously shared his extraordinary knowledge of Thoreau's writings. Other staff members at the Concord Museum, especially Adrienne Donohue and Carol Haines, effortlessly—or so it seemed to me—attended to the details of the exhibition and catalogue publication.

In Chadds Ford, Brandywine River Museum of Art Director Thomas C. Padon encouraged my participation. Amanda C. Burdan, Associate Curator, Gail A. Stanislow, Manager of the Annenberg Research Center, and Carol Ellis provided valuable insight and assistance. I am particularly grateful to James H. Duff, Director Emeritus, for his comments on the final manuscript. In the Andrew Wyeth office, Mary Landa, Collection Manager, provided unqualified support; she and her colleagues Karen Baumgartner and Amy Morey addressed my every inquiry.

Will McGrorty of Pemcor and Art Kaplan of the Getty Conservation Institute shared their expertise in some of the technicalities of period printing techniques. And, as always, Michael Podmaniczky sustained my efforts in truly innumerable ways.

CHRISTINE B. PODMANICZKY

THE CONCORD MUSEUM IS GRATEFUL FOR THE GENEROUS SUPPORT OF THE FOLLOWING:

CATALOGUE FUNDER:
Wyeth Foundation for American Art

EXHIBITION LEAD SPONSOR:
J.P. Morgan

EXHIBITION CORPORATE SPONSORS:
Barrett Sotheby's International Realty
Carleton-Willard Village and Carleton-Willard At Home
Hart Associates, Inc.
McWalter-Volunteer Insurance/Pure Insurance
Skinner, Inc.

EXHIBITION SUPPORTERS:
Reinier and Nancy Beeuwkes
Michele and Alan Bembenek
Kate and Robert Chartener
Martha Hamilton
Anne Hayden and Ivan Burns
Gail Keane
Kathleen and Michael Kennedy
Jane and Jeffrey Marshall
Private Family Foundation

WITH SPECIAL THANKS TO THE EXHIBITION LENDERS:
American Illustrators Gallery
The Andrew and Betsy Wyeth Collection
Arkell Museum at Canajoharie
Boston Athenaeum
Brandywine River Museum of Art
Concord Free Public Library Corporation
Private Collections

SELECTED RESOURCES

The BRANDYWINE RIVER MUSEUM OF ART houses an outstanding collection of American art from the nineteenth and early twentieth centuries, and galleries dedicated to the work of N. C. Wyeth, Andrew Wyeth, and Jamie Wyeth. Located in Chadds Ford, Pennsylvania, the museum includes the Walter and Leonore Annenberg Research Center, the Andrew Wyeth Studio, and the N. C. Wyeth House and Studio. www.brandywine.org

The Brandywine River Museum of Art's N. C. WYETH, A CATALOGUE RAISONNÉ OF PAINTINGS, by Christine B. Podmaniczky, is an extensive compilation of detailed information regarding one of America's foremost illustrators and painters. The project, originally conceived by Betsy James Wyeth, the artist's daughter-in-law, was generously supported by the Wyeth Foundation for American Art and culminated in a 2008 publication. To explore the online version of the catalogue, visit www.ncwyeth.org.

Founded in 1886, the CONCORD MUSEUM is a gateway to the town of Concord for visitors from around the globe and a center of cultural enjoyment for the region. The museum's nationally significant collection of 38,000 objects includes iconic artifacts from Henry Thoreau's life, family, and community, such as his Walden Pond desk and bedstead, his surveying tools, walking stick, flute, snowshoes, and spyglass. www.concordmuseum.org

Five of N. C. Wyeth's *Men of Concord* panels hang in the Thoreau Room of the CONCORD FREE PUBLIC LIBRARY. The first was given in 1947, the gift of Ruth and Caleb Wheeler in memory of their son, Caleb Kendall Wheeler, who died in action during World War II. The Library Corporation purchased two additional panels in 1947. In 2003, the family of Emilie Norton Thomas placed two more panels in the Library in her memory. Related holdings include letters between Ruth Wheeler and Wyeth and rich Thoreau collections. www.concordlibrary.org

The FARNSWORTH ART MUSEUM, in Rockland, Maine, celebrates Maine's role in American art, including the art of N. C. Wyeth, Andrew Wyeth, and Jamie Wyeth. Their work is regularly on view as part of the museum's collection, and in changing exhibitions in the Wyeth Center and the Wyeth Study Center. www.farnsworthmuseum.org